BREAKING SHACKLES

THE AFRICAN-AMERICAN MALE MANIFESTO

DR. MORRIS CLARINGTON

Printed in the United States of America
First Printing, 2016

ISBN-13: 978-1519620835

ISBN-10: 1519620837

For Questions Contact:

Conceptual Integrative Solutions Global, LLC

1-912-495-8745

www.weseesuccess.com

I dedicate this book to my son, Cayden Morris Clarington. The dream of any good father is the wish that his son becomes a better man than himself. This is my wish for you Cayden. I know that I'm far from being a perfect man, but hopefully I will always be the perfect father. Be proud of who you are and find your purpose. You were born to shine and your light will change the world. Let no one convince you that you lack the potential to be anything less than great. I love you!

Table of Contents

Chapter 1:
What's the Problem?

Being a success coach, I'm asked frequently how I can lecture to other ethnic groups about success and leadership when there are clearly so many racial barriers challenging the success of African-Americans. I typically give a poised smile and reply, "That's why I'm an expert. I had to learn how to be proactive instead of reactive. Do not judge me by my successes. Judge me by how many times I fell down and got back up again. In order to get to where I am, I've had to overcome mountains of adversity, show character in the midst of ignorance, stand firm with courage in the face of intimidation, and be humble enough to recognize and correct my inadequacies."

In the discovery process however, this question raised a very critical need that I aim to address in this book. Building toward African-American male success means understanding ethnic differences and highlighting the problems that are specific to African-Americans. It also means reflecting on ways for African-American males to shape themselves given the unique problems they face.

According to W.E.B DuBois (American sociologist, historian, civil rights activist, Pan-Africanist, author and editor), African-Americans have at least two life-altering experiences in their life: the moment they realize they are Black and the moment he or she becomes aware that being Black poses a problem for some. I've had to learn to love my skin and not because of anyone else's perception of it. I'm not blind or ignorant to the fact that African-Americans face more obstacles than Caucasians. In fact, I think African-American men face more challenges than any other group in America. African-American men represent America's success and failure. I fear that America's social and race relations are moving backwards instead of forward. It seems almost trivial, with all of today's advances and social reform, that something as miniscule as a person's skin tone affects how others perceive them in the world.

There are some that will deem my words a personal attack towards their race, gender, or belief system. I'm well aware that this book will be met with much scrutiny and criticism. We live in a time where being politically correct is popular. America has a tendency to demonize those that do not share mainstream views or opinions. We skate around issues, because we don't want to offend anyone. Yet, we do a disservice to those individuals that need our untamed voice to address problems or injustices.

I'm willing to stand and confess that there is a need for change in the nature of how African-American men are viewed in society. This book was written merely to identify the problems affecting African-American males, because I can personally attest to their obstacles. I ask that you view my efforts as constructive criticism. The first step in any problem-solving process is to recognize that there is a problem before developing strategies to remedy that problem. By acknowledging that there is a need for change in how society at large views African-American males, we begin to identify the underlying hardwiring and thinking that has been left to simmer in those who may have advertently or inadvertently institutionalized it with such devastating consequences.

If at any time you become offended or angered by my views or statements, be outraged enough to be part of the solution and not the problem. When reading, people have a tendency to add their own thoughts and tone to the message. Progress seldom comes from those with a tranquil demeanor.

My goal is to be informative, blunt, truthful, and direct. The issues I'm addressing are concerns Blacks regularly converse about amongst themselves. I'm simply broadcasting these concerns to the public. I know this might not make people comfortable, but this is the reality. You can disagree with my perspectives, but they can't be ignored. Someone has to deal with these ideas that people would prefer to sweep under the rug. The soul of social action is to recognize your mistreatment and demand better. As my parents used to tell my siblings and me when we were children, "Not all Blacks are good, and not all Whites are bad. You have to protect yourself around everyone." I've learned that this statement couldn't be truer.

It is not my intent to blame or cast stones at anyone. Focusing my attention solely on African-American males doesn't mean that I'm diminishing the challenges that other ethnic groups or genders face on a daily basis in America. Essentially, I'm interested in comparing and contrasting the differences primarily between Caucasian and African-Americans, because throughout American history the two racial groups' fates have been incongruously intertwined.

Caucasian Culture in America

The richest one percent of Americans control a third of the country's wealth. The richest ten percent of Americans control seventy-five percent of the nation's wealth. Predictably, the top one percent are nearly all Caucasians. These are the Caucasians that hold the power of influence in America; their ideas represent what will be embraced by the dominant culture. This group of predominantly Caucasian males disseminates the access to opportunity for the rest of society across all industries. These Caucasians in power, are the people who lobby for laws and contribute to political campaigns, control the media outlets, retain business managers who do the hiring for the majority of our nation's businesses, and donate to Colleges and Universities affecting admissions to higher education. These are the Caucasian males that set the rules for Americans to follow. Yet, they themselves are not bound by the same laws or guidelines.

Throughout history, Caucasians have represented the dominant culture in America. America's entire construct has been at best influenced by European design. Caucasians are a race of people having descended from European origins and are identified by their distinct physical feature of having light skin pigmentation, specifically White skin. The term "Caucasian race" is historically used to describe the physical or biological type of some or all of the populations of Europe, North Africa, the Horn of Africa, Western Asia, Central Asia, and parts of South Asia. The term "Caucasian race" was coined by the German philosopher Christoph Meiners. Meiners' term was given more circulation in the 1790s by Johann Friedrich Blumenbach (German professor of medicine and member of the British Royal Society), who is considered one of the founders of the discipline of anthropology. (Beckwith, Christopher (2009), Pearson, Roger (1985), Coon, Carleton Stevens (1939), Smay, Diana, Armelagos, Professor George (July 2000)).

The African-American Experience

What distinguishes African-Americans from other immigrant groups in the United States is that their ancestors didn't enter the country by choice. The vast majority of today's African-American population traces its ancestry to the slave trade from Africa. Over a period of nearly two hundred years, millions of Blacks/Africans were kidnapped or purchased and then brought to the United States of America.

I was born into a family of generational farmers and spent the majority of my adolescence tending fields and raising livestock. Interestingly, I was raised on and farmed the same plantation my ancestors worked as African-American slaves. The plantation house and slave quarters that existed during their time still remain standing intact today.

Unlike most African-Americans, I can trace my lineage as far back to my oldest known maternal ancestor's arrival into America as a slave from the Senegambia region of West Africa. He was a young adolescent boy that would later be given the name Wash Davis. He was purchased from a slave auction in

Charleston, South Carolina by a Caucasian man by the name of William Mazyck Davis. Davis purchased two young adolescent slave boys that day: Wash and Earl Davis.

Davis would become their Master, while Wash and Earl would work and reside on the Davis 400-plus acre plantation in Perry, Georgia for most of their lives. Master Davis later granted Wash his freedom as payment for building his plantation home based on his service as an architect. Eventually, Wash was granted the opportunity to purchase the freedom of other fellow slaves. He also bought two hundred acres of farmland from his former master, which allowed him to create a suitable life for himself and his family.

The Davis-Felton Plantation is significant in Georgia architectural and agricultural history. William Mazyck Davis was born on February 20, 1821 to John Gamble Davis and Martha Harriett McDonald. He passed away on January 6th, 1870 in Mossy Hill, Houston County, Georgia, USA. William Mazyck Davis moved from South Carolina to Houston County, Georgia, in the early 1850s in search of new cotton land. In 1854, he purchased the major portion of his new plantation, and by 1864, he owned a considerable amount of property.

In 1859, Davis moved his family to the plantation, which was called Mossy Hill. The main house is a unique, early, and virtually unaltered example of domestic Italianate architecture of which very few survive from the pre-Civil War period in Georgia. Few Italianate plantation houses were built in the state during this time, and it has been suggested that the Classical tradition retained its dominance during this period because of its relationship to the increasingly adamant and strained defense of slavery. The Davis-Felton house thus survives as an excellent example of a little-practiced style in pre-Civil War Georgia.

According to Davis family tradition, William Mazyck Davis designed the house and oversaw its construction by his own skilled slaves and the slaves of his brother Edward. Davis was a major planter in Houston County. The slave census of 1860 records that he owned 94 slaves, while the 1864 tax digest lists the number of slaves as 110. The land has been in continuous agricultural production since that time.

During the Civil War, Davis organized and served as captain of Company H, Henderson Rangers, in the 45th Regiment. Immediately after the war, the Davis family, like many other planter families, suffered financial difficulties. Davis was declared bankrupt at the time of his death, and his land was sold in February of 1870 to his son, William Richardson Davis. The nominated property was owned by the Davis family until 1926, when it was purchased by William H. Felton. It thus represents an intact plantation owned by only two families since the 1850s.

African-American men and African-American women have survived in a country that for most of its history has been extremely inhospitable to them. Sure, there have been other immigrant groups that didn't want to relocate to America; they had to fight for their lives as refugees to escape persecution in their motherlands. Yet, no other immigrant group was forced as an entire race to relocate as were African-Americans.

African-Americans experienced further oppression of their values and language: to be denied agency for generations; to have their freedom, religion, and children taken away within a blink of an eye; to have everything that might unify them, as a person and as a group of people, intentionally destroyed and disseminated forever; and to have every fragment of esteem removed and inevitably replaced by the self-defeating themes of someone you're forced to call "Master." As a race, African-Americans have no identity other than a vast continent and no understanding of their heritage, other than what their Caucasian enslavers endorsed and from bits and pieces of oral parables their captured ancestors passed down to anyone courageous enough to listen. Every other group of Americans can admire the notion of their pioneer ancestors, fearlessly traveling across rocky seas or vast plains enthusiastic to create a new existence, put aside old culture, and adapt to the new frontier. Rebuilding a sense of identity for African-Americans is central to our times although the challenge is daunting given: our exposure to the dominant culture; the resulting crisis point that upcoming generations are experiencing; and ambivalence and misunderstandings by those African-Americans who feel threatened when they embrace and defend cultural norms that are rejected by the dominant culture.

African-Americans have worked relentlessly throughout history to make America home, proving their patriotism time and time again. African-Americans served as military personnel, even as America itself denied them their civil liberties. African-Americans proudly fought as soldiers to protect America and those aboard, even when: their own homes were being burned; their children and relatives were being murdered, raped, beaten, spit on, harassed; and they were denied employment and education.

What many Americans fail to recognize in our country's history, is that Caucasian soldiers enlisted and fought to protect their way of life in America, whereas, African-American soldiers enlisted and fought to change their way of life in America. African-American soldiers were fighting to break down barriers and to prove themselves as equals. Even though their ancestors put their lives on the line, it often seems as if African-Americans are still fighting to prove that they belong.

Returning to the original question about how I can lecture about success and leadership to other ethnic groups when I'm part of the African-American experience, it became apparent to me that I needed to help other African-American men confirm that their context was different. I embraced the need to orient my advice specifically to our struggle and compare our struggles to gain insights. This helps individuals who make similar observations and are struggling to stay true to themselves while experiencing how society marginalizes the critical issues surrounding identity.

Many Americans are in denial of how society really works. In fact, racial matters are such uncomfortable topics that book publishers like McGraw-Hill Education even attempted to desensitize the occurrence of the Trans-Atlantic Slave Trade. In one of their published *World Geography* textbooks (copyright year 2016), they sugarcoated the issue of slavery in a caption about immigration; they referred to Africans brought to American plantations between the 1500s and 1800s as "workers" rather than slaves. This caption received national attention when a Texas African-American teen's mother took to social media to confront the publishing giant. McGraw-Hill Education did correct the caption in the new edition of their textbooks, but the fact remains: it should have never been written, much less approved for publishing.

I assume one of the best things about being Caucasian in America is not ever wondering if the things that happen to you are because of your race. Yet, if you're an African-American in this country it can be difficult to distinguish if your race is influencing how others are treating you. Often times for African-Americans, life feels like a game of chess: Whites move first and then African-Americans are permitted to move. African-Americans have to respond to the moves that Caucasians initiate and gain advantages when they're available.

Many of the obstacles or problems that African-American males face can clearly be attributed to the legacy of slavery and discrimination that continues to influence our social and economic standing, as well as the residual psychological effects of this game of chess. There are problems impacting African-American males rather than a problem with African-American males. Unfortunately, the bigger and the blacker they are, the more problems they face, because people regard their presence as intimidating. Even the label of being called "African" American or "Black" provides a basis for social classification. This categorization or description compels individuals to recognize African-Americans by their physical features and then treat them accordingly.

Why place racial labels or emphasis on the type of Americans any of us are at all? The fact that African-Americans are referred to as "African" at all is a sign of the limited explanation of their history. Many African-Americans disassociate themselves from "Africa" particularly because of their lack of personal connection to the continent and cultures associated with it. African-Americans are a unique

American group. They have different traditions, different shades of color, and certainly different values.

Many people have trouble defining who they truly are. Factors such as race, gender, culture, country origin, sexuality, interests, traditions, ancestry and occupation can all play a role in a person's identity. But when these things come into conflict with one another, a person may feel as if they are torn inside. They may feel as if they have two separate identities or that their identity is divided into multiple facets.

Unfortunately, those who are multiracial or biracial have to bear the internal burden of scrutiny from being both African-American and their other ethnicities. One of my nieces is Mexican and Black, another one of my nieces is White, German and Black, but their fathers—my brother-in-laws—are both African-Americans. Although my nieces are multiracial or biracial, they are "African-American" by American standards, because of the "Blackness" of their skin. Their African ancestry seems to overshadow other lineages; they are considered African-American by default. It's because of this truth that they will experience the double consciousness that comes with being African-American. Although America has labeled them as African-American, they will have to decide which group they identify with the most and hope to be accepted into that group.

In the book, *The Souls of Black Folk*, W.E.B. Du Bois essentially defined Black America in the twentieth century with his notion of "double consciousness." It was the idea that African-Americans experience everything in this world both as Americans and as Black people. He believed that African-Americans have a metaphorical "veil" that covers their faces; this is why African-Americans can usually understand Caucasians a lot easier than the reverse. Double consciousness essentially means that as both an African-American and an American, they will have to choose when it's appropriate to be either. African-Americans are encouraged to suppress their cultural influence at work, at school, and in public for the risk of intimidating other races. Like Superman, they have to "put on" their Clark Kent persona in order to be deemed acceptable, appropriate, and non-threatening to the outside world.

African-Americans have to be mindful of their behavior every time they step out the door, no matter their age. As children, most Americans can identify with their parents telling them they need to behave a certain way in public. African-American parents socialize their children to not make waves, to not come up against the authorities, and to not speak impolitely when there are Caucasians present—particularly if there are Caucasians who possess influence.

I can recall growing up in rural Georgia hearing Black folks talk about "THE WHITE MAN" or "THE MAN" and how he was set on making the quality of life for African-Americans difficult. It wasn't clear to me in my youth, but as I grew older I realized that this illusive "WHITE MAN" or "THE MAN" that Blacks commonly referred to as if he was the boogie man was no distinct person at all. They were referring to a social construct that serves to benefit some groups and marginalize others.

Northern Urban vs. Southern Rural Racisms

Many Americans have no clue that there was a "Great Migration" that took place in African-American history. The "Great Migration" was a mass exodus of six million African-Americans that spanned most of the twentieth century. These African-Americans fled North to seek better wages and work, protection of the law, and an escape from Klansmen.

The northern urban African-American experience is certainly different from the southern rural African-American experience. In fact, it seems that most of the research done about African-Americans has been about their adaptation or maladaptation to the urban environment. Although African-Americans share the same ancestral homeland, they can't be more different from each other. Since they are different people, their life experiences are different. Education, wealth, and social/political connection are all factors that influence the African-American experience.

Growing up in the Bible Belt of the South, I understand the vital role religion plays in the daily decision making process of individuals. Southern rural racism is often based in religious fundamentalism. Racism is the fruit of prejudice. I think the difference between northern urban racism and southern rural racism is that southern racists are often times more upfront and unapologetic about their position or behavior. I think decades of being bombarded with images of a White Jesus has fostered the idea of White supremacy. It was supposedly God/White Jesus that sent the early settlers to America to take the country from Native Americans and ordained slavery. African-American slaves had no other choices but to pray to the only savior they were allowed to accept: "Jesus." Jesus was perceived as White, because the dominant culture in America identifies him as such.

For African-Americans, the Christian faith has been a source of comfort and pain. In America's past, Christianity provided African-Americans with sentiments of hope, forgiveness, and strength during turbulent times of their enslavement and fight for civil rights. While their wives and daughters were being raped and their husbands and sons were being whipped at the stake, hosed, bitten by dogs, and trampled, the notion of hope, forgiveness, and prayer were at their disposal.

Decades later, African-American descendants have preserved and adopted the ideologies of the Christian imposed faith, ingraining it into the very fabric of their identity and culture. Many present-day African-Americans still recognize "Jesus" as being White. If you were to visit some of the rural black churches in the South today, you can still see images of White Jesus on paper fans and other graphics dispersed throughout the church. This is just another example of the long term psychological effect slavery has had on African-Americans.

It is not my intent to diminish the value of Christianity. Bible text depicted Jesus as a Jew, and based on the hot desert climatic conditions of the region in which he existed, there's no possible way he could have been fair-skinned. If Christianity is indeed your desired faith, I would like you to consider the degree of God's divine power. Being all-powerful, God could have chosen to present Jesus to the world in any fashion he saw befitting. To assign a definitive color, gender, or race to Jesus is to place limits to his omnipotence, omniscience, and omnibenevolence. I think a lot of people confuse the idea of God/ Jesus with the government.

Racism in the North exists, except without the slower accents and the confederate flags. Northern racists are more casual in their approach to racism. Northern urban racism is based more on exclusion and stereotypes. Northerners tend to cover their racism with liberal politics and sensibilities. I think a common consensus amongst Caucasian liberals is that they like the idea of African-Americans, but they don't necessarily want them around (in their communities, homes, country clubs, or social circles).

The Essence of America

The very essence of America was founded on the religions, traditions, and customs brought over by diverse Caucasian immigrants from their ancestral homelands. Immigrant groups have come to America willfully with: their identity; their unity; their purpose; their agency; their families; their beliefs; their folklore; their education; and their self-love intact—independent from their experience of discrimination in this country. Immigrants know what they are facing, since they are willing to undergo the hardships they face in the process of being assimilated.

The average Chinese, Indian, Mexican, Korean, or Jewish immigrant isn't usually the average person from their respective country.

Inner Black Experience

Along with looking at how African-Americans compare with other ethnic groups, the social dynamics within the African-American culture can appear complicated. When I address my fellow African-Americans, when I refer to myself as Morris, I'm accepted as one of them. Yet, when I refer to myself as Dr. Clarington, they immediately shut down or dismiss me, because they assume I can't possibly relate to them. It's perceived that I'm excluded from the same day-to-day issues that affect them. No African-American should have to attempt to prove to anyone, including other African-Americans, how "Black" they are. Just because a person either didn't grow up in certain conditions or walks or talks differently doesn't mean they're more or less Black than any other African-American.

Breaking Language Barriers

People today know that racial oppression, discrimination, and stereotyping occur, yet when asked about it, they deny that it happens, because it is such an uncomfortable topic to discuss. Let's face it. Discussions about racial issues make many Caucasians uncomfortable. Many will simply nod politely. Some will attempt to change the subject. Some will excuse themselves from the subject and leave to avoid offending African-Americans. Some Caucasians think the best way for them to avoid confrontation with African-Americans is to not associate with them at all in social settings. They assume this greatly reduces the chances of being misunderstood or mistrusted.

Unfortunately, ignoring the issues doesn't help change things. I'm sure they would have more to say if the discussion was between them and another Caucasian. African-Americans learn early that race is not the kind of thing they can chat about with just anyone.

Often times when African-Americans attempt to enlighten the public about incidents of prejudice, injustice, oppression, or disadvantages in American society, they get accused of "playing the race card," "asking for handouts," "cynically seeking to absolve themselves of social responsibility," or "complaining too much." Some conspiracy theorists even go as far as to state that the reason Obama became President was because Caucasians wanted African-Americans to stop using the excuse that Blacks can't get ahead in America, because of racism.

Oddly enough, many African-Americans are reluctant to report incidents of racism and discrimination, because they: don't want to be ostracized; don't want a target on their back; don't want to be viewed as a problem starter; can't afford a lawyer; fear it may harm future employment opportunities; have no clue how or who to report the occurrence; or fear being fired. You would be surprised how many racial occurrences go unreported.

It especially hurts when those around you refuse to acknowledge it. African-Americans don't want other ethnic groups to discount their experiences or tell them that they're being too sensitive, especially by Caucasians. The message African-Americans typically receive is that White people don't want to hear it. They disregard their race as influential to their experiences when, in truth, they primarily benefit systemically, professionally, and socially from their race. It's a circumstance numerous Caucasians become so accustomed to, it can be challenging for them to see a different experience for anyone else.

Racism and Bigotry as it Exists

Legislation has enforced bans against explicit racism that have helped to hinder direct outward expressions of prejudice against African-Americans over the last several years. The Fourteenth Amendment extended citizenship to African-Americans and forbade the States from taking away civil rights. The Fifteenth Amendment prohibited disfranchisement on the basis of race. Still, forms of implicit racism, including symbolic racism, aversive racism, and ambivalent prejudice, have replaced these obvious expressions of prejudice. In fact, African-Americans have been the primary targets of racist discrimination for one of the lengthiest and continuous periods in the entire history of the human race (Joe R. Feagin).

Americans say times are changing for the better and that the racial issues that plagued African-Americans in the past are diminishing. Yet, way too often we open newspapers, listen to the radio broadcastings, or turn on our televisions, only to find out that another African-American has fallen prey to the hands of injustice caused by racism and bigotry that still exist.

African-Americans have never been a violent race of people. They have endured and maintained composure under the most horrific circumstances. Throughout America's history, African-Americans have been portrayed as the aggressors. Throughout history, the image that has been propagated by the media has been the armed malicious African-American committing crimes against the defenseless innocent Caucasian. Paradoxically, it has been African-Americans that have been victims of perpetual violence in America by Caucasians. Since their beginning here in America, African-Americans have endured immeasurable generational pain and suffering. Seldom have African-Americans retaliated with violence. The media overly exaggerate their acts of violence to create mass panic and a mischaracterized history in the White community. This mass hysteria gives those in power justification to pass and enforce discriminatory laws, all for the sake of maintaining alleged civil order.

I strongly believe that violence begets violence. And it rarely leads to a final solution. Yet, it's upsetting to hear Caucasian politicians in the media tell African-Americans that, "They must choose nonviolence in their struggle for equal rights and to trust in the law." These Caucasians can't presume to tell those who are watching their loved ones killed how they should react to discrimination they know nothing about. It's easy to say be nonviolent when you're the aggressor.

Ironically, Caucasians in power prefer for African-Americans to follow the American Baptist minister, activist, humanitarian Reverend Dr. Martin Luther King, Jr.'s philosophy because it's "nonviolent" and less threatening than the alternative. In fact, the media deemed Reverend Dr. Martin Luther King, Jr. the leader of the African-American Civil Rights Movement.

Whereas the militant philosophies of the American Muslim minister and a human rights activist Malcom X, the African-American political activist and revolutionary Dr. Huey Percy Newton, and American political activist Robert George "Bobby" Seale instill fear. All of the men mentioned above were considered terrorists by the United States Government. Today's Black Lives Matter movement has been labeled as a terrorist movement, just like the leaders and organizations that fought for African-American Civil Rights were in the past.

Today, those Caucasians in power are frustrated, because they can't name a Civil Rights Leader. They want to know who is leading today's fight for social change. They're asking themselves who can they zero in on and focus on and talk to. There are no Jesse Jacksons, there are no Al Sharptons, and there are no national leaders they can zone in on. Since they can't pin somebody down and make them the target of all their criticisms, of all their conversations, and their analyses, they fear the power of the "People's Movement." There are young leaders all over the place, therefore it's hard to pinpoint just one.

Episodes of unjust treatment and violence due to racism frequently go ignored. Many times the individual(s) that fall victim to these injustices are African-American males. African Americans' first interaction with police in America was defined by brutalities perpetrated by enforcers of slavery laws. Police brutality continues to be a haunting issue for Black America.

The following occurrences are just a few incidents that captured national attention.

- *On February 4, 1999, **Amadou Diallo**, a 22-year-old dark-skinned immigrant from Guinea, was shot and killed by four plain-clothed New York City Police officers outside his Bronx apartment. Diallo was unarmed at the time of the shooting.*

- *On Nov. 25, 2006, **Sean Bell**, a 23-year-old African-American male from New York City, walked out of a Queens nightclub after celebrating his bachelor party, climbed into his car with two friends, and died from fatal gun shots wounds fired by a group of five police officers.*

- *In 2009, **Oscar Grant III**, a 22-year-old African-American male, was killed by a Police Officer who unholstered his pistol and shot Grant in the back. The bullet entered his body, exited through his torso, and ricocheted off the platform back into Grant's body. The officer supposedly mistakenly fired his gun instead of his Taser.*

- *In 2009, **Victor Steen**, a 17-year-old African-American male from Pensacola, FL, fled from officers, was tasered, crashed his bicycle, and was run over by a police vehicle.*

- *On January 29, 2010, **Aaron M. Campbell,** a 25-year-old African-American male from Portland, was shot and killed after he emerged from his apartment where officers had been called to check on a suicidal armed man. One officer believed Campbell was reaching towards his pants for a gun. However, Campbell was unarmed.*

- *On February 26, 2012, **Trayvon Benjamin Martin**, a 17-year-old African-American male from Miami Gardens, Florida, was fatally shot by George Zimmerman, a neighborhood watch volunteer, in Sanford, Florida. Zimmerman claimed that Martin looked suspicious and decided to pursue him.*

- *On January 11, 2013, 17-year-old **Kendrick Johnson's** body was found rolled up in a wrestling mat in the gymnasium of Lowndes High School, Valdosta, Georgia, where he was a student. A preliminary investigation and autopsy concluded that the death was accidental. Johnson's* *family had a private pathologist conduct another autopsy, which concluded that Johnson died from blunt force trauma.*

- *On July 17, 2014, **Eric Garner**, a 43-year-old African-American male from Staten Island, New York City, died from chest compression when arresting police officers placed him in a chokehold.*

- *On August 9, 2014, **Michael Brown**, an 18-year-old African-American male from Ferguson, Missouri, was fatally shot by Darren Wilson, 29, a White Ferguson police officer.*

- ***Steven Eugene Washington**, a 25-year-old autistic African-American male, was shot by Los Angeles gang enforcement officers after he approached them and appeared to remove something from his waistband. Police investigators reported that the victim was unarmed.*

- ***Tamir Rice**, a 12-year-old Cleveland boy, was fatally shot by a police officer. The officer allegedly thought the replica handgun the youth had in his waistband was real.*

- *Nine members [(**Tywanza Sanders** (age 26), **Clementa C. Pinckney** (age 41), **Sharonda Coleman-Singleton** (age 45), **Depayne Middleton-Doctor** (age 49), **Cynthia Marie Graham Hurd** (age 54), **Myra Thompson** (age 59), **Ethel Lee Lance** (age 70), **Daniel Simmons** (age 74), **Susie Jackson** (age 87)] of the historic Emanuel African Methodist Episcopal Church in downtown Charleston, South Carolina, were massacred by a 21-year-old gunman Dylann Roof who was seeking to kill "Black people." The victims were attending Bible study during the time of their deaths.*

Good old-fashioned racism is alive and well, as many adhere to the ideology of a social order where Caucasians alone are at the top of the hierarchy. In today's world, it's not easy to identify racists, because many of them no longer run around in white hoods and sheets, but they still exist. Just like most things evolve over time, they too have evolved in their actions. Discrimination in the United States is often thought of as one group actively oppressing another. It's been reported that the most common place to experience racism and discrimination is at work or school. The word "discrimination" invokes visions of hostile acts.

When most people think about or report incidents of racism, they think of inequality in terms of being denied access to an opportunity, position, or service. This discrimination includes: being treated a particular way based off of a racial stereotype; enduring an antagonistic work environment; or experiencing a deviation from what has been established as the norm. Some characterize their experiences as a form of harassment, such as verbal assault or profiling.

However, many people overlook subdued forms of racism. Social scientists have described microaggressions as "the new face of racism," declaring that the nature of racism has changed over time from explicit expressions of racial hatred and hate crimes towards expressions of docile racism, such as in-group favoritism or microaggressions that are more elusive, abstruse, and often inadvertent. This has led some Americans to mistakenly assume that racism is no longer a serious problem. Studies show that a wide variety of people in the United States experience these types of racisms.

In an article published in *American Psychologist*, social psychologists Anthony Greenwald and Thomas Pettigrew identified, that discrimination results more from helping ingroup *(your own race)* members than from harming outgroup members in America today. The question isn't really about who is oppressing whom *(another race)*, but rather about how: through our acts of kindness, we are unintentionally driving segregation, racism, or contributing to discrimination.

Rev. Dr. Martin Luther King Jr.'s words heartbreakingly express America's current truth. "The majority of White Americans consider themselves sincerely committed to justice for the Negro," he wrote in the 1967 book, "Where Do We Go From Here: Chaos or Community?" "They believe that American society is essentially hospitable to fair play and to steady growth toward a middle-class Utopia embodying racial harmony. But unfortunately this is a fantasy of deception and comfortable vanity."

Racist outcomes can arise simply through the human tendency to help people with whom they share something in common. This explains why there are so many disparities between racial groups despite the facts that explicitly racist policies have been outlawed and public-opinion censuses have shown a huge jump in racial tolerance in recent years. It's human nature to help those with whom we share commonalities. The problem is that, because of how stubbornly persistent segregation is in most facets of American life, "something in common" tends to have a racial component.

Racial microaggression may be subdued or unintentional. However, this doesn't mean that its effects are less detrimental. I find that many Caucasians are quick to see racism in others, but slow at owning their own. Having said that, most people don't think about it, but the most segregated places in America are the Baptist and Methodist churches on Sundays today.

Examples of Microaggression:

- Assigning intelligence to a person of color on the basis of their race. **The statement of racial microaggression:** *"You are a credit to your race." "You are so articulate."* **The message that is conveyed:** African-Americans are generally not as intelligent as Caucasians. It's unusual for someone of your race to communicate well.

- Statements that indicate that a Caucasian person does not want to acknowledge race. **The statement of racial microaggression:** *"When I look at you, I don't see color." "Race doesn't matter." "We're all the same in God's eyes." "America is a melting pot."* **The message that is conveyed:** I deny a person racial/ethnic experiences. Stop complaining and deny your individual heritage and assimilate to the European culture.

- The notion that the values and communication styles of Caucasian culture are ideal. **The act of racial microaggression:** *Dismissing an individual who brings up race or culture at work or school setting.* **The message that is conveyed:** Leave your cultural baggage outside.

- <u>A person of color is presumed to be dangerous, criminal, or deviant on the basis of their race.</u> **The act of racial microaggression:** *A Caucasian man or woman clutching their purse or checking their wallet as an African-American approaches or passes. A storeowner following an African-American customer around the store. A Caucasian person waits to ride the next elevator when an African-American is on it.* **The message that is conveyed:** You're a criminal / You're going to steal / You do not belong / You are dangerous.

- <u>A statement made when Caucasians deny their racial biases.</u> **The statement of racial microaggression:** *"I'm not a racist, because I have Black friends."* **The message that is conveyed:** I am immune to racism, because I have African-American friends.

- <u>When Caucasians refuse to acknowledge an African-American education or prestige title.</u> **The act of racial microaggression:** *They refer to the individual as Mr. or Mrs. while knowing, or after being corrected, in regards to the addressing of their prestige title. They use the excuse, "I call everyone by their first name, or by Mr. or Mrs." They assume it's okay to address an African-American by their first name, Mr., or Mrs., without consulting them as to their preference. They make light of the African-American when correcting them in regards to addressing their title, implying that an African-American is being overly sensitive.* **The message that is conveyed:** I neither care about nor respect your title, nor will I address you by it.

- <u>Statements that assert that race does not play a role in life successes.</u> **The statement of racial microaggression:** *"I believe the most qualified person should get the job." "Don't blame me for what my ancestors did." "All that racist stuff happened in the past, but things have changed now." "Everyone can succeed in this society, if they work hard enough."* **The message that is conveyed:** African-Americans are given unfair benefits, because of their race. People of African-American descent are lazy and need to work harder.

- <u>Occurs when a Caucasian is given preferential treatment as a consumer over an African-American.</u> **The act of racial microaggression:** *An African-American is mistaken for a service worker. Having a taxi pass an African-American and pick up a Caucasian passenger. Being ignored at a store or attention given to a Caucasian customer that entered after you.* **The message that is conveyed:** African-Americans are servants to

Caucasians. African-Americans couldn't possibly occupy high-status positions. You are likely traveling to a dangerous neighborhood. Caucasians are more valued customers than African-Americans. You don't belong.

(Adapted from: Wing, Capodilupo, Torino, Bucceri, Holder, Nadal, Esquilin (2007). Racial Microaggressions in Everyday Life: Implications for Clinical Practice. American Psychologist, 62, 4, 271-286)

I've had several experiences with racism. I learned earlier on as a teen that when African-American teens congregate, it's commonly perceived as problematic. It's presumed that they somehow pose a threat to public safety or are conspiring to commit an illegal act. It's no secret to African-Americans that a group of Black males riding in a vehicle together is more likely to get pulled over by law enforcement than their Caucasian peers.

Growing up in a rural town, there wasn't much for teens to do as it related to entertaining themselves. Most of the time, teens found enjoyment in hanging out with each other in parking lots or restaurants. The teens typically chose to hangout in parking lots where businesses were no longer up and running. I can recall how Caucasian police officers would treat African-American teens differently from Caucasian teens. When African-American teens would go to a parking lot and hangout, the police officers would tell us to break it up and go home. When we would ask why, they would often convey, "Because we were loitering or because they told us so!" We were astounded by their actions, because it wasn't like we were drinking or causing a public disturbance. Heck, we were all good teens. Many of us were "A" students and participated in local sports.

Even when we received permission from local business owners that it was okay to congregate outside their respective establishments, police officers would make it their business to make us disperse if they were on patrol. The upsetting part was witnessing many of the Caucasian teens in parking lots hanging out in the same way as we were—not even a mile down the street—when we were forced to leave. Yet, there were no police officers seemingly present to break up their interactions.

This was a blatant racial biasness to many of the African-American teens, but because we were teens at the time, no one took our accusations seriously.

As an adult, I've been in restaurants with my Caucasian peers and the quality of my customer service by the Caucasian waitresses or waiters was far less than suitable in comparison to my Caucasian peers' experience. Once, I attempted to be tolerant toward a Caucasian waitress for her actions, because I didn't want to cause a scene. In fact, I attempted to mentally rationalize her actions, in an attempt to avoid perceiving the matter as a racial issue. However, her actions became quite obvious to everyone in the group. Ironically, it was one of my Caucasian colleagues that addressed the waitress and brought her lack of proper service to the attention of the restaurant's management.

My Caucasian peers were very apologetic, but it wasn't their fault. It was no more their fault than it was mine. I explained to them that I was fine, but they had an opportunity to witness first-hand the racism that African-Americans encounter on a regular basis—racism that many Caucasians are blind to or naive about.

I shiver when I attempt to fathom the scope of racism my ancestors endured in America. My experiences with racism could never equal that of theirs. Yet, the pain I experienced from racism hurts all the same. My most horrible racial encounters occurred as an adult during my graduate school experience. I attended a predominately White graduate school in the Blue Ridge Mountains foothills of South Carolina. The recruiter for the college made me aware prior to my acceptance that it was a Predominately White Institute (PWI) and that he was charged with the task of increasing African-American student enrollment. My enrolling class would have the largest population of African-Americans entering in the college's history.

Upon initially entering the college, I noticed that the faculty, staff, student body, and graduates were primarily Caucasians. It didn't bother me, considering that I spent most of my life being the only African-American in many extracurricular programs and during the course of my educational career. I also figured that if prestigious Caucasian families were willing to send their relatives there, then the college must have a well-respected reputation amongst the social elite.

Although many of the individuals were welcoming, there were a few that resented the presence of African-Americans. I think many of the Caucasian students took our presence as a hostile takeover. There were wisecracks made by some of the Caucasian students such as: "I never intended to enroll in a Historically Black College or University (HBCU);" "The quality of my education will now be diminished by their presence;" "I will now have to keep my belongings closer;" and "There goes the neighborhood." There were also subtle forms of microaggression exhibited.

Some of the faculty and staff members were no better than the students, as it related to their prejudice and racism towards African-Americans. After getting to know many of the Caucasian students, I was shocked to learn that many of them had never gone to school with African-Americans. It was because many of them were from prestigious families that sent them to private schools, PWIs, or attended undergraduate online. You could tell that many of them seemed uncomfortable in our presence and viewed African-Americans by media stereotypes. Some of the Caucasian students and faculty members were flabbergasted by the degree of our knowledge; in fact, they were so astounded that they accused us of cheating.

I can recall an occurrence where a few of the African-American students and I all received letters in the mail that there would be an Academic Honor Council hearing held in three days in which the state of our continued enrollment would hang in the balance. We had been accused of cheating by a group of our peers. The college would decide if we were guilty or not. I considered these measures to be a bit extreme. I had known of incidents where Caucasian students were caught cheating at the college. Academic dismissal was never the first disciplinary action by the school's administration in those incidents. Yet, academic dismal always seemed to be the answer when dealing with the school's "black problem." The

African-Americans had served their purpose at the college. Now, there were those at the college who were ready for us to leave. The African-American students were there simply to increase minority enrollment so the college could obtain federal subsidies.

The feelings that passed through me were surreal. All I could think about was how hard I had worked and the sacrifices I had made to get to that level of education. It appeared that my life had flashed before my eyes. I was insulted, but worse, I was hurt. How or why on earth would anyone accuse me of cheating? I had made it this far on my own wits and knowledge. Why on earth would I change things now? What would I tell my parents? Better yet, what would I tell everyone in my small rural town that was rooting for me to succeed? I presumed an accusation of this nature would follow me the rest of my life if I didn't have it cleared.

My head was spinning in an attempt to make sense of this accusation of cheating. To me, there must have been a logical explanation for the mistake. Maybe someone had taken a body gesture of mine out of context, or maybe I stared across the room too long during an exam? Maybe it was God testing me? My mind was puzzled with *what-ifs*.

Days prior to the Academic Honor Council hearing, those of us who stood accused had an opportunity to converse amongst ourselves. I was enlightened to learn that the reason why we were singled out for cheating was because we scored the highest grades on an exam. I can remember giving a puzzled look to everyone, then a cynical snicker.

Venting to the group, I uttered, "What does that have to do with anything? Instead of condemning us, they should be congratulating us. When I was failing, no one came to encourage or provide me with assistance. Now, when it finally seems like I've figured out how to properly prepare and do well, I get accused of cheating. It's one thing after the other, here at this school."

After calming down, I immediately went to the office of the Caucasian professor who taught the class where we were accused of cheating. I felt an urgency to clear my good name. I knew the hearing was only a few days away, but the possibility of being expelled from school made me anxious. I didn't feel I could wait another day. My nerves were in a fret and getting a good night's sleep was out of the question.

After speaking with the Caucasian professor, I was astounded to discover that he was on our side. He stated that the accusations were preposterous, but his hands were tied, because the families of the students that made the accusations of cheating held strong ties with the college. The Caucasian professor stated confidentially that he perceived their accusations as a sign of racial jealousy. After leaving the Caucasian professor's office, I immediately shared parts of our conversation with the fellow accused. The group decided we needed to address the college's upper administration before the close of business that day.

When we attempted to speak with someone from the college's upper administration, everyone refused to see us. The front office assistant was ordered to relay a message from one of the upper administrators to us. She stated that we should not approach our accusers, because this action would be perceived as intimidation, and could result in immediate dismissal from the college, or charges being filed with law enforcement officers.

It was the Caucasian professor that stated that we should seek legal representation, because the matter clearly had racial motives. We took his advice and asked the NAACP to come to our aid. On the date of the hearing, the college's all Caucasian upper administration and the student accusers were surprised that we had gone to the extent of calling the NAACP to protect our interests.

When the hearing was finally called to order, the hearing officers asked what led to the accusation of cheating. The response from one of the administrators was that, "There is no actual proof of any of them cheating, but these students couldn't possibly have done as well on the test in question as our better students."

Most of those in the room were astounded by the notion. The President of the NAACP chapter stood to his feet and asked him to clarify. Being asked to repeat the question, I guess the gentleman thought about what he was saying and became apprehensive. He decided not to repeat the statement on grounds that his statement would be misinterpreted. Yet, everyone in the room, Caucasian and African-American, knew what he meant.

Since the administrators refused to repeat the statement, the President of the NAACP Chapter condescendingly paraphrased it, "Because these African-American students' grades were higher than their perceived smarter Caucasian peers, they must have cheated." Things from that point pretty much went downhill for the administration. One question followed another, including, "What made the Caucasian students better students?" The next question was how students could make accusations of cheating when the professor himself failed to recognize that any cheating took place. Before the NAACP left the hearing, the college was practically begging the NAACP not to contact the press or have African-American students file a lawsuit.

After that incident, many of the African-American students at the college decided to transfer to other colleges. I chose to remain. Those African-American students that chose to persist with me pledged that we would hold each other accountable for achieving success. As a result, we formed a support system that allowed each of us to graduate.

I can recall another incident where a racist Caucasian professor of mine, who also served as Academic Dean of the college, persistently recorded the wrong grades for my tests and assignments. If it had not been for me making copies of everything I submitted to her, I might not have graduated.

Intuition urged me to go to her office at the end of the academic term. I had a hunch that something wasn't quite right, so I asked if the Professor/Academic Dean would state to me the grades she intended to submit to the Registrar. I wasn't surprised that all the grades she had listed for me were failing. Realizing her mistake,

I immediately attempted to reason with her. Her demeanor was stern and cold towards me. She accused me of lying and attempting to negotiate my grades. The Professor/Academic Dean stated that these were the grades I had earned, so these were the grades I would receive. She attempted to belittle me, stating that everyone wasn't cut out for higher education or certain careers. When she was done insulting me, she asked me to leave her office. Before leaving, I reached into my bag and retrieved duplicate copies of my graded assignments. I didn't see a need to say much more. I politely thanked her for her time and shut the door to her office.

I could have easily went into her office and acted hostilely. I assumed this would have been the behavior she desired and expected from me. She would have been happy to suggest that an argumentative demeanor was typical for a Black man. But I would not give her the satisfaction of making me act out of my pleasant character. Knowing her personality, she would have easily made herself the victim in the situation anyway. I found gratification in my calm demeanor. I walked out of her office happy that I kept my cool, despite the circumstances.

I didn't bother reporting the incident. Besides, after showing her proof of her mistakes, she had no other choice but to correct her grading errors. Even if I had told someone, chances were that no one with any leverage at the college would believe me. In the eyes of my Caucasian peers and her fellow Caucasian colleagues, her ethics were unsurpassed.

It wasn't clear to me until after I had graduated, why the Professor/Academic Dean expressed ill will towards me. I concluded that she was intimidated by Black male intellectuals. I was the worst type of Black person as far as she was concerned. The Professor/Academic Dean perceived me as an "uppity nigger", this was because I didn't fit any of the negative Black male stereotypes. She had come to realize that my knowledge and skills were equivalent and possibly exceeded that of her own; allowing me to graduate would only confirm that notion. So, she attempted everything within her power to hinder my success. Upon graduating, I would possess the same degree and title as she had earned. No longer would she be able to internally validate her racial feelings of White intellectual superiority.

Caucasians are often blind to racism, because they've never had to experience it. There are some good-hearted Caucasians that have naïvely abetted racist Caucasians in fulfilling their hidden agendas. They do not see the true nature of the person. Racists who wear white sheets are easy to spot. Those who cloak themselves in good deeds are well camouflaged. I can remember confiding in one of my Caucasian friends and telling him that a former Caucasian professor of ours was racist. I knew he was rather fond of the professor, so I was somewhat reluctant to disclose this information. To African-Americans, it was obvious that everything about his demeanor screamed racist. His private comments to African-Americans in the confines of his office confirmed our feelings. When I told my friend, I couldn't convince him that the Caucasian professor was a racist. Naively he defended the Caucasian professor saying that he couldn't be a racist, because he had never been racist toward him. I simply smiled and told him not to be so ridiculous. Weeks later, sure enough, a fellow Caucasian faculty member heard a recorded conversation of the Caucasian professor making racist comments about one of the African-American female students.

When I reminisce with my fellow Caucasian colleagues about their former graduate school experiences, they laugh and smile about the delightful years at our alma mater. They chuckle about the lavish dinners and poolside parties at our former Caucasian professors' and classmates' homes. They chat about their fondness for our former professors and how much they miss them. They converse about the humorous encounters with inebriated classmates and discreet run-ins with the law. To them, these were some of the best days of their lives. The stories from the African-Americans consisted of years of tears, struggles, prejudice, racism, and sacrifices. Our experiences were the complete opposite of those we shared the classroom with daily. If you didn't know any better, you would have thought we went to different schools.

Ultimately, many of the Caucasian students became my friends. They realized their actions and apologized for their initial behavior towards me. I think they admired my unwavering desire. No matter the number of obstacles thrown my way, I never retreated. Nor did I walk around feeling sorry for myself. Every day, I was at the college sitting front and center, ready to take on whatever else the college threw at me. Eventually, attitudes of resentment became sentiments of acceptance. More faculty, staff, and students started to include me in their inner circle. I guess they figured, "if they couldn't beat me, then they might as well include me." Their actions proved to me that people are capable of change.

My decision to stay at the college didn't come easy. I stayed because I didn't want those that sought to hinder my success to have the satisfaction of saying they made me run away. I wanted them to see me graduate and witness my success. I wanted them to remember that I stood firm in the midst of adversity and triumphed.

Considering everything that happened to me while I was at this college, if given the opportunity, I wouldn't change anything about my experience. No one likes to experience racism, but like the old saying goes, "What doesn't kill you makes you stronger." My experiences at the college made me realize quite a few things. For one, I learned that the world was unsympathetic and unapologetic. I learned to have faith, be disciplined, and to remain focused on the end goal. I also learned that as a Black man, my excuses would always fall on deaf ears. The world would grant me no leniency. At last, I learned how to dot my "i's" and cross my "t's," to speak well, smile, hold my head up, have tough skin, and to work well with those that may not personally like me.

Obstacles within the Context of Finding Success

As I look at the beautiful Black faces of my own children, I ponder in fear how they will be greeted by the world. Life itself is filled with many obstacles and to think that their skin color might add to their challenges is a difficult burden for a parent to bear. Their sweet innocent youthful faces are covered with an oblivious bliss to the world around them. I question when or if I should tell them that their skin color might be the cause of prejudice or unfair treatment at some point in their life.

This is a common dilemma that all African-American parents have to face. When we have children to care for, the world looks different from when we have none. When we are poor, the world looks different from when we are rich. It's no denying that our race plays a major role in our worldview. New experiences bombard each one of us daily and add to the nature of our perceived reality.

It's reasonable to hope that parents desire to prepare their children to functionally exist. My wife and I have high expectations for our children, as all parents should. We want them to fulfill their purpose and enjoy a successful life. What type of parent would I be if I didn't warn them of the bigotry that exists in the world? They would be considered naïve and others would take advantage of them. It's my job to prepare them for the world.

On the one hand, I fear that divulging the realization of racism and discrimination might stifle their ambition, or worse, lead them to make excuses. I would hate for them to blame or justify their failures by "playing the race card." On the other hand, disclosing the realization of prejudice and injustice might make them more conscious of their behavior and the actions of others. Some people would go as far as to argue that even mentioning racism or bigotry in itself is inadvertently teaching the idea. But if we decide to shield our children from this truth, what reasons do we give when our children encounter these injustices?

My personal experience has taught me that a tendency to avoid problems by ignoring the problem in the hopes that it will go away is in itself a major problem. What reason would I give to my daughter when she asks why she didn't get invited to one of her Caucasian classmate's birthday party with the rest of her Caucasian classmates, when clearly she's the only African-American student in the class? Do

I tell her that the real reason she wasn't invited was because her classmate's parents or relatives didn't feel comfortable in the company of Blacks? What reason would I give to my son when he asks why he didn't win the science fair at his predominantly White school with a panel of all Caucasian judges, when clearly he had the better experiment and presentation amongst all of the participants? Do I tell him that the reason he didn't win was because the judges and the winner's parents were in the same social circle and that influenced their decision? What reason do I give to my children for them being pulled over by a Caucasian police officer for no violation at all, yet they are questioned and asked to step out of the car? Do I tell them that everyone is treated this way and the officer was just following standard protocol?

Within the Black community there has been much talk about bringing about a change to every person of color, and while the methods to bring about this change are constantly debated, many Black people (myself included) agree that a change is needed. To say that the election of Barack Obama is major progress and African-Americans have triumphed over years of oppression is like saying that he's the first Black person that has been qualified to be President. For decades, Blacks have qualified to lead our country. African-American males led the Civil Rights Moment; they run their homes, businesses, hospitals, and colleges every day. Barack Obama's candidacy was just the first time; many outside of the African-American race entertained the idea of a male of color as President of the United States. Not to be condescending, but that's not African-American progress, that's non-black America's progress. Don't get me wrong. I love and respect President Obama. He's had to cross racial barriers many of us would tremble in the face of during his political rise to presidency. His election made African-American boys and girls across the county dream they could become anything they desired. Therefore, I praise President Obama for being a symbol of hope and inspiration.

Our country as a whole should be proud that mainstream America finally saw that electing a person of color for the Presidential position was fitting. What the President did for Americans is introduce the concept that race should not matter. Yet, his term has been a bittersweet reverence, considering that during his entire term, the Republicans were the majority of the House. It seemed that his ideas were trampled before they could blossom into something great. Also, let's not forget that there were more publicized incidents of African-American men treated unjustly during his term in office since the Civil Rights era.

Many of us hope that the problem of racism and discrimination will go away on its own. Almost all of us, to a greater or lesser degree, attempt to avoid problems. We procrastinate, hoping that problems will go away. We ignore them, forget them, and pretend they do not exist. We attempt to skirt around problems rather than confront them head on. Or we hope that someone else will take on the challenge and we all benefit from their labor. This is nothing shy of what the past generation of civil rights leaders encountered.

Not all African-Americans were welcoming to the idea of standing against the injustices of that era. The African-American civil rights leaders of the 1950s and 1960s had doors slammed in their faces and were threatened by the same Black communities they attempted to serve and protect. Much of the reluctance of older African-Americans of that period to stand against the racism and discrimination was due to fears, the fear of: being fired from their jobs; property vandalized; being physically attacked; or their families becoming targets. However, history has proven that injustice is always within arm's reach. Injustice most often finds us. When people stand by idly when injustices occur, it's only a matter of time before injustice hits home and then a sense of responsibility and urgency is expressed.

Much of the discrimination that occurs today results from unconscious stereotypes that are not widely understood and from negative stereotypes that mainstream media and less-than-credible statistics or so-called "reputable research" has depicted to the public. Often times, other ethnic groups have preconceived notions or opinions about African-American males prior to being exposed to them. African-American males are characteristically depicted as: poor; angry; manual labor/blue collar workers; having an absent or uninvolved fathers; uneducated or struggling in school; loud with terrible grammar; only good at sports (football, basketball, track); headed toward a life of disadvantage; deviants; or criminals. If that's not enough, the negative portrayals of African-American males have evolved.

These preconceived notions stemming from negative depictions of African-American males cause potential employers to overlook them for career or advancement opportunities. African-American males are portrayed as lazy, childlike, immoral, and unintelligent. Caucasians are portrayed as hard-workers, sensible, intelligent, virtuous, and compassionate. Despite fancy legal jargon about every employer being an equal opportunity employer, discrimination still exists in the workplace, but now it's done more discreetly than in the past.

Even when it seems African-American males have crossed racial barriers and earned leadership positions in esteemed careers, it seems it's difficult for other ethnic groups to accept their position of authority as their superior. There's an inconceivable amount of backlash that questions, undermines, or criticizes their position of authority or qualifications. Other ethnic groups are in disbelief, because they perceive the advancement of the African-American male to be a personal attack on them.

Although African-American males are faced with many challenges, they should not let it deter or discourage them from striving for excellence. Most African-American males have heard since birth that they will face complex systemic barriers to opportunity. Furthermore, they've heard that they are: more likely than any other ethnic group or gender in the nation to live in the most disadvantaged neighborhoods; more likely to begin life under the most problematic conditions such as grow up in poverty; more likely to become victims of violence and poor health; and more likely to be raised in single parent homes with limited resources.

African-American males' inadequacies have been overly exaggerated. I'm not saying there isn't a problem. The problem is that when African-American males allow themselves to become victimized, they allow for others to make excuses or rationalize their failures. Far from the popular belief, the majority of African-Americans aren't looking for a handout, but a hand-up from disparities. Granted, African-Americans are the descendants of slaves and they still have a greater deal to overcome, because of their oppressive past. However, such a past does not constitute a handicap.

There are many reasons for these social economic gaps, but there are also many intertwined solutions. African-American males seem to know more about why they fail, than why they succeed. The result is an unbalanced depiction that overemphasizes their deficiencies and neglects to pay attention to the assets and strengths they bring to the table. It's important not to focus on the disadvantage gaps of African-American males, but on the opportunity gaps that exist. Focusing on disadvantage gaps does more harm than good, because it sets limitations. Once African-American males have surpassed what statistical data has set forth as their obstacles, they lack the desire to excel further. In other words, African-American males become content with good and they never seize the opportunity to become great. African-American males don't have the luxury of being just average or good enough. They must standup and standout. They must not settle for being average, because average has already been done. It's the exceptional people in the world that have the greatness impact.

I know what some of the readers are thinking: true, African-American males today are not completely denied of resources or opportunities. An African-American male can be wealthy, possess status, and be politically and socially well-connected. Some African-American males have risen above their circumstances, in spite of those that attempted to hinder their success, or to spite those that would attempt to hinder their success. However, rarely does mainstream imagery convey the accomplishments of African-American males.

I think each of us attempts to make sense out of the nonsense of the world. The question becomes how did the association of African-Americans being unappealing or evil transpire? Throughout history Black skin has become embodied with all the undesirable traits of humans. Think about all the negative associations with the concept of blackness, like the black-death, the black plague, black as sin, and the fear of the dark and death. In the movies, black is usually the color of evil. It's even worn by the bad guys. It's clear to see how black skin became associated with evil and why African-Americans became feared.

Hollywood movies perpetuate what those Caucasians in power want to portray. The money behind most Hollywood productions are older Caucasian men ages sixty and above. For far too long, African-Americans view the image of the self-loathing African-Americans female whose life is in shambles until she meets the successful Caucasian guy who saves her. Additionally, just the opposite is promoted with the image of the beautiful Caucasian woman who meets the African-American male and is dragged into a relationship, ruining her life.

Famous Heavy Weight Champion Boxer Muhammad Ali stated publicly his hatred of how movies always depict the guy in the black hat as evil, or how the black car stalls just before reaching the finish line, and the white car crosses the finish line just in time to win the race. It is a strange sensation, this double-consciousness—this sense of always looking at one's self through the eyes of others and of measuring one's essence by the opinions of a world.

Even when African-Americans name their children they have to have this double-consciousness. It's perceived that names of European descent, or a.k.a. "Christian" names, are more appropriate. It makes no sense that African-Americans should have to deny family names or their cultural uniqueness in fear that their children will be denied equal employment opportunities due to discrimination based off of association of name and color. A name has nothing to do with a person's ability to perform a task well. African-American males mistakenly pride themselves on the passing of last names to their children that do not reflect their family legacy of origins.

African-American police officers are more conscious when dealing with Caucasian violators of the law, because they realize their actions will be more scrutinized. This is a double-consciousness that Caucasian police officers typically lack. Because of the strong political ties many Caucasian families possess, their leadership often undermines African-American police officers' authority.

The late Dr. Ja A. Jahannes stated to me once, "That it is the responsibility of African-Americans to empower their own culture by flooding the world with their music, books, plays, art, products, and businesses. African-Americans can set the stage for how the rest of the world views them. Realize that you are a part of the fate of Black men and our stereotypes. Either you will be a part of fixing it or making it worst. Therefore, think before you open your mouth. Be aware of the power your words have and use them wisely and be articulate. Take care of your personal appearance as well." The power of African-American males lies in their unity and their ability to recognize a need for reform. Empowering themselves doesn't mean they should seek or desire the oppression of other races, nor does it mean they should avoid helping to strengthen others, regardless of their color, race, or creed.

I think a lack of communication causes much of the ignorance that surrounds racism and discrimination. As I stated earlier, many of us form our opinions about other racism and cultures based off of the media's depiction. Many of us have never interacted with other races outside their workplace, school, businesses or the restaurant settings. It's no secret that many of us are not our typical selves in these settings. African-Americans exhibit this double-consciousness, as I stated earlier. They are usually more refined and on their best behavior. In truth, ask yourself: how closely do you interact with other races outside of these settings? How many times have you invited those from other races to come to your home on a typical day and hangout? I think the disconnect happens for some of us when we lack a basic understanding about the reasoning behind the other person's worldview.

Caucasians often accuse African-Americans of causing all uncomfortable matters or confrontation about race. However, it's difficult for Caucasians often to understand, because they are born with an even slate. It can be hard to imagine that their African-American friend, neighbor, or coworker is living a completely different experience simply by virtue of their race. In an attempt to address that communication breakdown, I think of the wonderful movie *The Color of Fear*. It is a 1994 documentary that is powerful and discusses the experiences of individuals from different cultural backgrounds and how we all exist in a society that privileges Caucasians. Eight North-American men, two African-American, two Latinos, two Asian-American and two Caucasians were gathered by director Lee Mun Wah and writer Fabrice Guerini, for a dialog about the state of race relations in America as seen through their eyes at a weekend retreat in Ukiah, CA.

White Canadian author Margaret Atwood wrote a great short story that reveals the kind of act Caucasians put on when faced with "a person from another culture," as she puts it. It's called *The Man from Mars* and is part of a short fiction collection called "Dancing Girls." The main character is pursued by a man from "another culture." As Christine's relationship with this man evolves, her ideas about people from other cultures begin to surface. Her views result from her mother's ideologies and her social background. The story exposes prejudicial attitudes in an individual who thinks she's "done her bit for internationalism." From the beginning, Christine expresses a generally ignorant attitude towards people who are of a different cultural background from her. The two people in the story who expose her to different cultures are the man who is pursuing her and the servant girl.

It's easy to overlook things when the cards are in your favor. Whose "reality" do we define as the most real? Those that are the most visible? The most common? The most powerful? Instead of evaluating our own personal encounters and making generalized judgments about whether or not race plays a role in today's society, ask how many others from the same or different ethnic group encounter similar experiences, and what does this tell us about our own worldview and our society. This information can only be divulged through communication.

Everyone has a different worldview, so we can't expect a Civil Rights leader or any person other than ourselves to convey this message. We have to realize that there is no one person in a race of people that can express the feelings of everyone in that race. We are all different people with different needs and different concerns, so no race has a "spokesperson." This is also the reason why we can't stereotype an entire race by the actions of a few.

African-Americans must be willing to teach other ethnic groups about their culture and language, so they can effectively communicate and understand them. The Bible says, "Speak to the people in a language they can understand." In 1 Corinthians 14:10-13 it says, "There are many different languages in the world, and every language has meaning. But if I don't understand a language, I will be a foreigner to someone who speaks it, and the one who speaks it will be a foreigner to me. And the same is true for you. So anyone who speaks should pray also for the ability to interpret what has been said."

When we don't understand another person's language, or when that person doesn't understand ours, then a breakdown in communication takes place. Misunderstanding, confusion, even hostility can be the result. Caucasians do not understand the African-American experience. However, making a genuine connection with another person means empathizing, understanding, and being able to view the world through their eyes. Failure to communicate is for many people the single largest reason they can't get their point across. It isn't that they lack a suitable vocabulary, it's usually because they don't know how to use the right words at the right time.

African-Americans reside in a society that operates off of European culture, so obviously certain things don't feel natural. We all must attempt to remove color lines, but we must embrace our heritage. This will be difficult, because there is a fine line between the two. Many will pose the question: how can we as a nation remove color lines when each race is holding onto their culture. It's a matter of embracing the accomplishments of each other's heritage and seeing the equal value all ethnic groups have to offer.

Although every culture in this melting pot called America has something of value to offer, each group must be careful not to celebrate one culture's dominancy, oppression, or subjugation of another. In recent years, there has been much debate in regards to the Confederate Flags towering high and waving in the wind of public institutions in the southern states. Many African-Americans view the presence of these flags as a form of microaggression and detrimental to the advancement of people of color. However, Caucasian supporters of the flag publicly deem it as a symbol of "Southern Pride." Their position is that the flag celebrates the bravery and spirit of their Confederate ancestors. Yet, the flag represents a continuous painful reminder to African-Americans of the horrors of their ancestors' enslavement and persecution. The flag ultimately symbolizes to African-Americans the celebration of an army of individuals willing to die for the right to keep a race of people permanently enslaved.

By embracing your heritage, you show pride for the accomplishments of those ancestors that died and sacrificed for the luxuries you enjoy. Embracing ones heritage means embracing oneself, which ultimately means loving and having pride for one's self. The way you treat yourself sets the standard for others. When we are ashamed of ourselves, the cutting edge of our creativity atrophies. We tend to become so preoccupied with our own inferiority that we are unable to come up with new ideas. When we believe that whatever we attempt will fail, we may choose to avoid doing anything that isn't a proven success and relatively risk-free.

African-Americans must learn how to adapt without losing themselves. Consequently, African-Americans know more about their maladaptation than adaptation. It's not what we are that holds us back; it's what we think we're not. Like artists, African-Americans must learn the rules, so they can break the rules. If African-Americans are to incorporate the information they've ascertained, they must continually revise their course, and sometimes, when enough new information has accumulated, they will have a clearer view of the terrains in which they must cross. African-Americans can learn from their mistakes and triumphs. By doing so, they are able to break the shackles that hinder their socioeconomic advancement.

It is with this double-consciousness that African-Americans will be aware of Caucasian America's culture and how to assimilate into that culture and what it perceives as normal, while also conserving the uniqueness of their own culture, so they can relate to one another. There is no secret that middle- to upper-class African-Americans find it easy to assimilate into mainstream America. Generation X *(birth dates ranging from the early 1960s to the early 1980s)* may be the first group of African-Americans that actually experienced a more level social experience since slavery. Possibly, in four to five generations, African-Americans will be oblivious to the difficulties of race, as are most Caucasians. Today's millennial generation *(birth years ranging from the early 1980s to the early 2000s)* seems to be more open-minded and tolerant of change, but the racist echoes of their grandparents or great grandparents still seem to linger in the back of some of their minds. Though the millennial generation is more technologically advanced and receptive to change, they are a generation that has been handicapped and stifled in many regards due to their parents' constant coddling. Many of them lack key decision-making skills and possess a sense of entitlement. Let's hope that this generation will level the playing field for all Americans alike.

Chapter 2:
Breaking Misconceptions

The individual racist need not exist to note that institutional racism is pervasive in the dominant culture. Racism is embedded in the framework and organization of American culture. There are some Caucasians that will refuse to acknowledge or accept that they harbor racial prejudices. In fact, some will go as far as to say that racism no longer exists. When racial prejudice is not acknowledged, this can cause individuals to engage in conduct that disadvantages African-Americans without consciously realizing they are doing so. The discrimination occurs when it is not obvious to them or when they can point to a race-neutral justification for their actions. Racism can be an everyday fact of life for African-Americans, even if Caucasians care to recognize it or not. Overall, the reality for African-Americans is that Caucasians continue to wield disproportionate power and enjoy higher standards of living and our governments' power structure perpetuates their marginalization.

According to Debra J. Dickerson, an American author, editor, and writer on race relations and racial identity in the United States, Caucasians are victims of *"aversion therapy" in that they refuse to see their own complicity in racism. Furthermore, Caucasians "assume their perfection" and exhibit "a continued refusal to see America as inherently, organically multiracial and multicultural."* Dickerson asserts, *"That Caucasians' narcissism is only one leg in a historical conspiracy."* She wrote, *"Simply put, Whites held hands across generations to hold Blacks down long enough to ensure that their own heirs would ascend to as much privilege as possible while simultaneously keeping their hands clean."*

So when I read or hear older Caucasian politicians talk about getting back to the "Good old day" in America, I take their comments to be extremely offensive, considering America's past for African-Americans has been far from pleasing. When African-Americans walked down the street, they had to move because someone White was walking pass. African-Americans had to take off their hats or avert their gaze in the presence of Caucasians. Two hundred fifty years of slavery. Ninety years of Jim Crow. Sixty years of separate but equal. Thirty-five years of racist housing policy. If you ask me, this seems far from a pleasant living experience for African-Americans.

"Fear of something is at the root of hate for others, and hate within will eventually destroy the hater." (George Washington Carver).

Some people criticize whatever is different, because they are not accustomed to it. Many of these people are also very insecure, which explains why they are uncomfortable with people who don't look, think or act like them. But other factors are at work, as well. These factors include: media representations; individual upbringing; whether someone embraces a multicultural definition of America; need for social acceptance; our sources; perception; and an individual's set of insecurities and how they respond to them in and out of their comfort zones. We consider some of these factors, look at what negative stereotypes are being reinforced and developed, and explore the reasons.

We all have preconceived notions about other races and these notions often determine how we interact with those individuals from that race. Racial-ethnic stereotypes, including characterizations of communication and social skills, are often fashioned and perpetuated by the media. Stereotyping is the establishment of a mental image that is representative of a particular group, whereas individuals in that group are perceived as lacking individual uniqueness or possessing identical characteristics. When a particular behavior by a group member is seen, the viewer evaluates the behavior through the lens of the stereotype. This causes the observer to determine that the conduct has legitimized their stereotyped belief about that group. Stereotypes can be so deeply internalized that they persist in the face of facts that directly contradict the stereotype.

If there's one truth, it's that people aren't born racist, they are introduced to it, whether it is from a relative, a friend, the media, or an outside source. Think about how parents feel about race and then watch young children. Regardless of what the adult feels, those young children are fine with interacting with children or adults from any race. It's just not that encouraged. Instead, media representations and adults start to use what researchers like to call generic language. When used in storytelling, stereotypes are created in children's brains, according to researchers from New York University and Princeton University. They don't care about color. Most of the time they don't see a difference between them or the next person, besides obvious age, height, and gender. As it relates to other children, all they're concerned with is playing or having fun.

Even if a child does recognize that there's a color difference, it still doesn't make a difference to them. It's not until the parent(s) or someone connected to those children makes them aware of their color differences that they perceive "race." It also happens a lot because of silence. When children see and hear the news or drive through various neighborhoods and are exposed to racial profiling, they may start to believe that Whites and Blacks don't belong together in the first place, unless adults teach them otherwise.

White Skin Privileges

Some Caucasians might argue that their white skin didn't do anything to prevent them from experiencing poverty. Poverty-stricken Caucasians get upset when the word "Privilege" gets thrown around by African-Americans. People feel more comfortable diminishing racial matters to class-based ones, assuming that poverty explains most, if not all, of the differences between the African-American and Caucasian experience. But for African-Americans that possess a degree of wealth, issues of poverty are not the problem.

Many times, Whites in poverty get discriminated against because of their poverty. Most times a college education can even tip the scale in their favor. A college degree doesn't necessarily open the same doors for African-Americans from impoverish conditions. Poverty influences everything about your perspective on opportunities for advancement in life. Middle-class educated people assume that anyone can achieve their goals if they work hard enough. Folks steeped in poverty rarely see life in this opportunistic manner.

I understand that people can be privileged in some ways and definitely not privileged in others. There are many different types of privilege, not just skin color privilege that impact the way people can move through the world or are discriminated against. These are all things you are born into, not things you earned, that afford you opportunities others may not have. Recognizing privilege simply means being aware that some people have to work harder just to experience the things others take for granted.

Yet, it's impossible to deny that being born with white skin in America affords people certain unearned privileges in life that people of another skin color simply are not afforded. Caucasians are ordinary human beings, accustomed to a skin privilege they refused—and continue to refuse—to acknowledge. Society has taught Caucasians that being colorblind is the best they can do, and so they never explore the ways in which skin privilege and cultural differences can lead to a system of race-based oppression and a completely different way of seeing the world. Viewing the world as if you're colorblind takes away the beauty of God's creativity.

Caucasians typically spend very little time thinking about what their own race means to them. Many Caucasians navigated the world with a lack of racial self-awareness as "White." Instead of understanding that their whiteness has all sorts of significance in their life, they are taught to see themselves as merely individuals. Caucasians are oblivious about the significance of their own racial status.

Although Caucasians and African-Americans experience the world in two very different ways, this is not said to make White people feel guilty about their privilege. It's not their fault they were born with white skin and experience these privileges.

It's not unusual for African-Americans to wonder how different their lives would be if they were White. "If I were White, maybe I would have gotten that job, gotten that promotion, gotten out of that traffic ticket, gotten a better deal on that new car or house, paid a little less on those repair costs, gotten a grade of an "A" instead of a "B" in that course, gotten better seats in a restaurant." African-Americans asked to sit on interview panels commonly wonder about the true nature of the request for their presence. Are they being asked because their employer values their opinion or because they're a Black minority asked to sit amongst their fellow White colleagues to show the candidate that they're an equal opportunity employer?

James Baldwin wrote in a letter to his nephew, *"There is no reason for you to try to become like White people and there is no basis whatever for their impertinent assumption that they must accept you. The really terrible thing, old buddy, is that you must accept them. And I mean that very seriously. You must accept them and accept them with love. For these innocent people have no other hope. They are, in effect, still trapped in a history which they do not understand; and until they understand it, they cannot be released from it."*

Media

The media shifts the way we see the world. The media shapes many of our worldviews, belief systems, and values and provides models for appropriate behavior and attitudes. Think about it, the media depicts the "appropriate" roles of men and women, parents and children, or bosses and workers. Media depicts what defines "success" and how it is achieved. Media depicts what qualifies as "criminal activity" and what are the sources of crime and social disorder.

Mainstream media holds the power to reinforce dominant social understandings of race and gender, which further produces a discriminating social system. Mainstream media never hesitates to inform the public of another African-American male menace arrested for gang violence, drugs, theft, assault, or murder. It often appears that if an African-American male does find social, political, and financial success, there is always someone waiting to slander his character.

The media infiltrates our thoughts by repetitively displaying these stereotypical illustrations through various forms of media artifacts. For example, how many times have you seen a Black neighborhood displaying alcohol signs in a highly visible spot near a market? What causes this aggressive marketing in the neighborhoods: demand, the placement of the signs, or depictions that accept that these signs are part of the neighborhood and not to be disputed, since it might bring revenue? As a result, they become more commonly accepted as truths or indisputable realities that are too uncomfortable to discuss in mixed company.

The media sells both products and ideas, both personalities and worldviews. The notion is that mainstream media products and cultural values are fundamentally intertwined. Our media has helped create a belief system that assists in justifying the actions of those in power by often times distorting and misrepresenting reality. Racism has historically been one of the most prominent American cultural frames and has played a major role in determining how other ethnic groups perceive and behave toward African-Americans.

It's fair to say that mainstream media seems to be a facilitator and sometimes a source of social problems. African-American males are defying their negative stereotypes every day. Media sources are the major influence on society's denial and the cause of many African-American male stereotypes. The media implies that all African-American males are as seen on TV, music videos, or the news. When I examine the imagery conveyed by mainstream media, I'm not so much interested in the specific activities depicted in a single newspaper, movie, or hit song as in the broader system of meaning of which these depictions play a part. When you tune in to your local or national news, what do you see? Or more importantly, who do you see? Do you see the media depicting an African-American making a fool of him or herself while being interviewed? It seems reporters seek out unintelligent, negative stereotypical portrayals of African-Americans. This is apparent in the different ways Caucasian subjects and African-American subjects are portrayed.

These depictions are intended to create and reinforce stereotypes about African-American culture. Popular media outlets largely remain predominantly White. Missing diverse perspectives from the media landscape can have wide-ranging detrimental effects. The type of coverage that gets chosen by Caucasian editorial staffs then reinforces negative stereotypes rather than clarifying the news. African-Americans make up over thirty-five percent of the U.S. population but hold just over seven percent of all radio licenses and three percent of all TV licenses.

There is often time a lack of accurate coverage by the media. When African-Americans are excluded from conversing with the media, other people tell their stories, or the stories remain untold altogether. In turn, the media reinforces negative stereotypes of those communities; this is the problem of predominantly White controlled media outlets.

A Hollywood Diversity Report authored by Dr. Darnell Hunt and Dr. Ana-Christina Ramón looked into film studios' executive ranks in 2013. They discovered that ninety-six percent of the CEOs and/or chairs were Caucasians. The report also found that approximately ninety-three percent of senior management in these film studios were Caucasians. A study by the Cooperative Children's Book Center at the University of Wisconsin found that of 3,200 children's books published in 2013, only sixty-seven were authored by African-Americans, and only ninety-three were centered on Black characters. According to publishers, one major reason there is a lack of diversity in children's books is that titles featuring Black characters in primary roles don't sell as well as ones with White characters, and so aren't picked up by publishers. The question becomes why?

No other medium has the ability to reach so many American homes, influencing personal opinion, ideas, and racial attitudes, than the news, magazines, radio, Internet, and television. Think about how your dreams and ideas of the world are subconsciously shaped by media ads, television shows, movies, music, social media, and other persuasive programming. It is through these persuasive mediums that negative stereotypes develop and have resulted in fear, alienation, exclusion, ostracism, joblessness, and intense punitive treatment in public schools and the criminal justice system. Everyone belongs to at least one group that is characterized by some sort of stereotype.

Any of us who intend to do very much in life will have to accept the fact that there will be times when we will not receive approval from everyone. Regardless of how wonderful we are as individuals, there will be those that will dislike us, fear us, or distance themselves from us because of negative stereotypes. They are more comfortable maintaining their mindset, even if they have never challenged any of their concepts or stereotypes, because that's what they know. Breaking their idea of 'who they are' is part of building your success.

Not the Same Fight

There has been a considerable amount of attention paid to Lesbian, Gay, Bisexual, and Transgender rights these days. I must point out that the battle for African-American Civil Rights and LGBT Rights are not the same. To compare the two forms of oppression is to diminish the role of racism in America, which manifests from a system of slavery that deemed African-Americans legally inferior by birth.

When I think about African-American Civil Rights, my mind takes me to the 1950s and 1960s Jim Crow era. It was an era when African-Americans couldn't vote, couldn't stay in hotels, couldn't eat in certain restaurants, but if you were White and gay, you could. Marriage equality does not prevent Caucasian Lesbians, Gays, Bisexuals, or Transgenders from their White skin privilege. Nor does it protect African-American Lesbians, Gays, Bisexuals, or Transgenders from the Black racial experience.

Need for Social Acceptance

African-American males are consciously and relentlessly working to offset negative stereotypes. Everyone craves acceptance. Therefore, criticism and judgment are hard on us mentally and emotionally. The fact is, it hurts to be criticized or judged. Criticism and judgment are often tools used to prevent any of us, no matter our color, from fulfilling our destiny and to steal our liberty and creativity. You can exhibit yourself so that you stand out from the negative stereotypes by: being humble yet confident in your abilities; being assertive in your actions; having a positive outlook and attitude about life; having effective body language; being able to adapt to any environment; working on your negative traits; and being aware that your language impacts your environment and those around you.

Negative stereotypes and misconceptions that need to be broken

While both African-American males and females are subject to racial profiling due to negative stereotypes, African-American men suffer a higher incidence of profiling and seem to be especially targeted, not only because they are Black, but also because they are males. When African-American males are disproportionately labeled, this allows the unleashing of an extensive range of legal discrimination measures in employment, housing, education, public benefits, voting rights, jury duty, and so on.

Here's a list of the few negative stereotypes associated with African-American males:

- African-American males are always running from law enforcement.
- African-American males blame all their problems and failures on other ethnic groups, especially "Caucasians."
- African-American males have terrible grammar and speak poor or broken English.
- African-American males are terrible or absent fathers.
- African-American males invented the fashion trend, "Sagging."
- African-American males are lazy, lack motivation, uneducated, loud, and unemployed/underemployed.
- African-American males are always looking for handouts.
- African-American males lie, cheat, and steal.
- African-American males are angry and aggressive. Their demeanor is uninviting. (If you're a Black male who doesn't smile much, it makes other ethnic groups nervous. I learned earlier on in life that smiling seems to make Caucasians particularly comfortable.)
- African-American males typically live in poverty-stricken areas.
- It's perceived that African-Americans tip poorly or not at all.
- African-American males are dangerous and deviants. (This also affects how law enforcement approach and interact with males of color.)
- African-American males have gang affiliations.
- African-American males only listen to Rap and R&B music.
- All African-American males are great athletes.

As I stated in Chapter One, African-American male inadequacies' or deficiencies have been exaggerated. I want to point out a few of the statistics that many have accepted as truths about African-American males that are completely incorrect.

- **Fewer than fifty percent of African-American males graduate from high school.** The high school dropout rate for African-American males is narrowing; not only are they graduating, but they are transitioning into higher education.

- **African-American males fail to matriculate to our colleges or universities.** The percentage of African-American males enrolled in higher education has risen. In fact, the percentage of increase for African-American male student enrollment outweighed that of their Caucasian counterparts.

- **We've all heard the statement that there are more African-American males in prison than in college or at universities.** In actuality, there are more African-American males in college than in prison.

- **African-American males are terrorizing our Black communities and killing each other will little regard.** "Black-on-Black crime" was a term coined in the 1980s used to depict the increase in gang violence in urban communities. Since then, the expression has been used to perpetuate the impression that there is an epidemic of in-group violence in the African-American community that's not exhibited in other ethnic communities. There is no evidence that African-American males kill each other at a higher rate than other groups. In fact, most deaths can be attributed to a perpetrator who is the same race as the victim.

- **African-American male students are treated and disciplined in the same manner as their non-black peers in our school systems.** The American school system treats African-American males unfairly. African-American male students receive a disproportionate number of suspensions, detentions and have a much higher rate of being expelled from school.

- **African-American male students have the same opportunities as their peers.** Public schools, where the enrolled student populations are predominately African-American, have less access to experienced teachers and advanced placement classes. The Annie E. Casey Foundation, a private philanthropy based in Baltimore and working across the country, recently found that African-American students face the highest obstacles to opportunities. The foundation's researchers evaluated success across twelve benchmarks, including literacy proficiency, income, rates of employment, among others. The report concluded that when African-Americans were compared to other racial groups using these benchmarks, they performed far worse due to various disparities.

- **African-American male students lack ambition and are underachievers.** Distorted data has fabricated the idea that African-American male students are unmotivated and are underachievers. A research study showed that African-American students improve their grades after having the assignment expectation reinforced by their teachers.

So the question becomes, where did the data regarding these widely accepted statistics come from? It's the so-called "researchers" and their affiliates, which are reporting the statistics about African-American males that are driving the ideology of the "Black male in danger." They've figured out how to capitalize off the proclamation to tackle these issues affecting African-American males. They open up businesses/nonprofit organizations and go into our colleges, communities, social organizations, prisons, and businesses and charge a substantial fee for their data and expertise on how to address solving African-American issues. Not only do they receive compensation for the previously stated institutions, but they also receive federal and state grant moneys and receive charitable donations from other companies.

These companies are more than willing to throw money or free products and services their way, considering it's a tax write-off for them. These big companies can now say to the public that they've contributed to the advancement of minorities. It makes perfect business sense. There's a great deal of money to be made from painting the disadvantaged African-American male picture. Therefore, those that capitalize off of this "Black male in danger" notion will always make sure that the data portrays that they are deficient and disadvantaged. The "Black male in danger" stats are outdated, but many still attempt to hold them as truths.

The Effectiveness of African-American Male Initiatives

Although there are quite a few program initiatives aimed at providing support to African-American males, the impact has been minimal. Those that choose to serve the Black community must be active for the right reasons. No one should choose to serve any civil rights endeavor to be rewarded, worshipped, or praised. Marcus Garvey stated, "Leadership means everything—pain, blood, and death."

Many times the programs to assist African-Americans are impractical to implement especially when it comes to how to address the issues facing the populace. Their so-called "help organizations" seem to be more about promoting their name or becoming their own boss, without making any real change in the Black community. They are content with sitting in conferences and conventions in four or five star hotels, and talking about what they will do, while they award plaques to speakers.

It's my opinion that African-American males need more counselors and mentors. Mentors can help give individuals knowledge, cope, and form strategies so that they can become successful.

Perception

Why is it that the stereotypes surrounding Caucasians are so much more positive and those centered on Blacks are negative? Caucasians are perceived as being: smart; possessing excellent grammar; hard workers; happy; family-oriented; financially comfortable; ambitious; great leaders; and possess money. African-Americans aren't completely absolved of their role in fostering some of their own negative stereotypes. Although, don't forget that no person can truly represent an entire race. When you're in the presence of others outside your ethnic group, they see you as a representative of your entire race. It seems when some Blacks open their mouths publicly they set the entire African-American race back two hundred years.

Refuse to accept the negative opinions and limiting comments of others. *"Truth is not only violated by falsehood; it may be equally outraged by silence."* (Henri Frederic Amiel) African-American males need to lend their voices to clear these misconceptions and stereotypes. Stop letting ignorance be spoken in front of you. It's necessary for African-American males to express their anger. Moreover, African-American males must possess the capacity to creatively express their anger without violence or hatred.

"He who can modify his tactics in relation to his opponent and thereby succeed in winning may be called a heaven-born captain." (Sun Tzu)

The injustices that result from negative stereotypes warrant anger, especially if you've been: looked over/passed over for opportunities; unjustly treated; antagonized; or belittled. Yet, it is how African-American men handle these adversities that sets the stage for how the world perceives them. African-American men need to act differently than what is expected of them. If African-American men engage people with what they expect, then they are able to discern and confirm their projections. Being criticized is not a problem if you develop a positive way of dealing with it.

"If evil be spoken of you and it be true, correct yourself, if it be a lie, laugh at it." (Epictetus)

Again, it's okay to be angry, but smile and plan to overcome.

"Love the man that can smile in trouble that can gather strength from distress, and grow brave by reflection. Tis the business of little minds to shrink, but he whose heart is firm, and whose conscience approves his conduct, will pursue his principles unto death." (Thomas Paine)

Marcus Garvey wrote, *"If the Negro is not careful he will drink in all the poison of modern civilization and die from the effects of it. So they must be careful what they choose to believe about themselves.*

According to Frederick Douglass, *"I didn't know I was a slave until I found out I couldn't do the things I wanted."*

I too, didn't realize I was supposedly disadvantaged until I read in a book somewhere that Black males were an at-risk population group. It's like when you're poor, you don't know you're poor until someone tells you otherwise. This is most likely because everyone around you is also poor. African-American males must be careful not to let the ideology of being disadvantaged hold them back. They must not let the ideology handicap them.

"Before we can properly help the people we have to destroy the old education...that teaches them that somebody is keeping them back and that God has forgotten them and that they can't rise because of their color...We can only build... with faith in ourselves and with self-reliance, believing in our own possibilities, that we can rise to the highest in God's creation." (Marcus Garvey)

A "Typical" White Person

Unfortunately, most Caucasians don't put themselves in a position in which they can learn about African-Americans on a more personal level. So,

African-Americans find themselves placing Caucasians into categories of "typical" and "atypical," albeit unconsciously.

President Barack Obama once spoke on race at the National Constitution Center in which he referenced his own White grandmother and her prejudice. Obama stated that she was a "Typical White person." Of course, President Barack Obama received plenty of criticism from the media in regards to his statement. The general public believed his remark to be offensive and racists. His comment got me thinking, what are the perceived attributes of a "Typical White person?" This question led me to create an opinion survey that would poll a random group of three hundred individuals on what they considered to be "typical" characteristics of a White person in the United States. I was rather surprised by the results, considering the majority of the sample population indicated that they were from Caucasian descent.

Since I live in Georgia, I wanted to make sure that my sample population was extremely diverse, so I had my team interview one hundred individuals from Warner Robins, one hundred individuals from Columbus, and one hundred individuals from Hinesville. I intentionally chose these towns because they're major military towns in Georgia. The results from my survey concluded the following:

Characteristics of what's perceived as "Typical" Caucasian mannerisms.

- Desire to be in control of their environment
- Win at all cost: "Everything is a competition"
- Must always "do something" about a situation
- Passive Aggressive
- Speak authoritatively and condescendingly
- Wealth equals worth
- Faith in Justice System
- Willing to share details of personal life with others freely
- Pretend to know it all (no matter their level of expertise on the subject)
- Heavy value on ownership of possessions and property

- Your job is who you are
- Adherence to rigid time schedules
- Time viewed as a commodity
- Christianity is the norm or "right" religion
- A woman's beauty is based on being thin, having full lips and big breasts
- A man's attractiveness is based on economic status, power, and intellect
- Husband is deemed breadwinner of household
- Animals seen as one of the family or human
- Inquisitive; willing to pry into someone else's personal life
- Willingness to confront those that reject or exclude them
- Medication solves all problems
- Avoidance of physical punishment as a disciplinary measure when rearing children

Every group has mannerisms people perceive as norms — patterned characteristics of behavior and communication. Often norms arise unintentionally, reflecting a culture, and may or may not convey a group's diversity. Positive and negative racial stereotypes are often derived from these supposed cultural norms. The sheer act of articulating cultural norms can expose the unintentionality of current group norms while also creating an approach to support an effort of change.

Chapter 3:
The Power of Education, "The Great Equalizer"

I often tell the young African-American males I mentor, that they must be committed to their education so that they can create a better future for themselves, their communities, and their country. Many of us have a common enemy, "It's the ignorance of our upbringing." This simply means that there are principles to success that many of us are not taught. I attempt to make them understand that circumstances do not define their future; life is but a series of decisions and education is intended to prepare us for life.

Racism in the public education system no longer takes the explicit form of segregated schools: White students spitting on Black students or National Guardsmen with rifles blocking the entrance to a school. Institutional racism is frequently subtle, unintentional and invisible, but always potent. Most of the racism in present-day schools is not born out of extreme hate and does not come from a place of wanting the worst for African-American students. Many African-American students, year after year, do not have access to up-to-date books, fully credentialed teachers, high-quality curriculum materials and advanced courses.

When African-Americans attempt to defy the educational boundaries set by White America, they are treated as criminals. In 2011, an Ohio mom, Kelley Williams-Bolar was sentenced to ten days in county jail, community service, and put on three years of probation for sending her kids to a better school district. School officials said that Ms. Williams-Bolar was cheating because her daughters were receiving a quality education without paying taxes to fund it. In addition those dollars needed to remain available to students within the district.

It's clear what lengths the school district went to catch Ms. Williams-Bolar driving her children into the district, because they hired a private investigator. School officials wanted to make an example out of her. The Presiding Judge acknowledged that he felt punishment or a deterrent was needed for other individuals who might consider defrauding various school districts.

Ms. Williams-Bolar experience is one of many that African-Americans face when attempting to better their children's educational experience. It's simple: school funding depends on taxpayer contributions. When you have an area were individuals are wealthy or middle class, the school district has better funding which equates to better schools. Poverty-stricken communities have less taxpayer contributions, which leads to less funding. Therefore, schools typically lack necessary books, better teachers, and equipment to facilitate learning.

The concept that education is a source of emancipation, a freeing of oneself from the limits of one's experience, has been around for centuries. Racist Caucasians are intimidated by African-American men who can read and articulate a position. Foul mouth, naive, simple, or overly aggressive Blacks have never been a threat to the status quo. In Frederick Douglass's autobiography, *Narrative of the Life of Frederick Douglass*, he explained how the wife of his owner taught him how to read in secret, and how her husband discovered what she was doing and scolded her for it. What his enslaver said to his wife is probably the most eye opening statements about the power of knowledge.

If you give a nigger an inch, he will take an ell. A nigger should know nothing but to obey his master — to do as he is told to do. Learning would spoil the best nigger in the world... if you teach that nigger how to read there would be no keeping him. It would forever unfit him to be a slave. He would at once become unmanageable, and of no value to his master.

For years, African-Americans were limited in their career growth opportunities and forced to accept jobs that Caucasians considered demeaning. In many instances, African-Americans were told they weren't qualified to get higher paying glorified jobs, because they lacked a college degree. So, African-Americans started to encourage their children to seek higher education. Booker T. Washington felt African-Americans should focus on building new schools that taught our young people useful job skills. These schools would help African-Americans lift themselves up the ladder of success. W.E.B. Du Bois felt that in education, African-Americans' main goal should be to increase the number of Black college graduates.

Showing Commitment to Education and Evaluating Its Merits

Education means to obtain knowledge or receive information. Many people possess a degree, but few are educated. During my years in higher education, I've noticed the value of education has changed. Now, it's more about money and convenience rather than knowledge and sacrifice. Many college graduates believe they're entitled to success, because they've obtained a degree. College only confers that a person possesses the ability to learn and think at a higher level; it doesn't entitle them to anything. I have come to realize that most people truly fail to understand the true definition of education. Education is not solely confined to being received in a teaching institution. You can become educated by reading literature (books, magazines, newspaper), watching documentaries, listening to audio, researching on the Internet, or by conversing with different people.

We live now in the "Information Age." African-Americans have gained the opportunity to read any book on any subject through the efforts of their fight for freedom, yet they refused to read anything outside the scopes of social media postings, articles or magazines about sports or celebrity gossip, or text messages. I read an article once that stated, "The best way to hide something from African-Americans is to put it in a book." Young African-Americans must read and gather information that they can apply.

Acquiring knowledge is vital to success and it doesn't necessarily have to take place in school. Education is a lifetime process, but people outsourced it to schools. An institution of learning is designed to verify that you have been exposed to critical thinking concepts. However, it is up to the individual to ascertain knowledge and utilize it beyond the capacity in which it was given. Knowledge must come first. You don't have to have a high IQ. Work with the cards you were given in life. Learning is only of value if it can be put to practical use. A degree is not indicative of being educated. You can be self-educated and make a greater impact on society than a person who has numerous accolades displayed on a wall or mantle.

African-Americans can only fight their way out of persecution by arming themselves with education. Degrees or credentials seem to validate African-Americans to other ethnic groups. It tells them that the Black they're dealing with possesses a certain degree of intelligence. Knowledge is power and education is the ultimate prerequisite for respect, political development, democracy and social justice. There is no progress or change without education. No illegitimate system can withstand the power of a well-educated majority.

When education lies within the hands of a few, they tend to maintain the status quo and impose a sort of cultural hegemony whereby the "mainstream" ideals of society are seen to be the correct ones. In Marxist philosophy, the term cultural hegemony defines the domination of a culturally diverse society by the ruling class, who manipulate the culture of that society, the beliefs, explanations, perceptions, and values, so that their ruling-class worldview becomes the worldview that is imposed and accepted. Under this influence, generations of African-American slaves lived under the impression that their master's best interests were their interests. In terms of applying a non-political lens to how we see which ideas are imposed onto African-American communities from a cultural perspective, I think ideas about what attributes define physical beauty, suitable names, what's considered an acceptable genre of music, appropriate fashion, and proper grammar or dialect are all clear examples.

The bureaucrats set on their disfranchisement feel secure: as long as the majority of African-Americans live in poverty and are bound by propaganda; as long as they lack higher education; as long as they can't network and engage in open exchanges with each other; as long as they murder themselves in the streets; as long as they confine themselves to debt; and as long as they lack upkeep of their communities.

"A little learning may be a dangerous thing, but the want of learning is a calamity to any people." (Frederick Douglass)

The power of education extends beyond the development of knowledge and skills. Education can lead to financial liberation and can contribute to nation building. Education can change lives, not only for the individuals ascertaining the knowledge, but for their children and grandchildren as well. That's one of the reasons why I love working in education. Unfortunately, not everyone has access to the education they so desperately need. There are still enormous inequalities in education in the United States.

Hidden Potential

While an education indeed was hard to obtain during the earlier years of America's history for Blacks, there were some that were able to break the color barrier. In 1799, John Chavis, a Presbyterian minister and teacher, became the first Black on record to attend an American college or university. Yet, there is no record of him receiving his degree from the college. The college is now known as Washington and Lee University in Lexington, Virginia. Later, in 1823, Alexander Lucius Twilight became the first known African-American to graduate from a college in the United States. He received a bachelor's degree from Middlebury College in Vermont. Earlier African-American intellectuals used their education to write and speak out against slavery and against racial inequality.

Many smart African-American young men today mask their intelligence by performing poorly academically, because of the negative peer pressure of their environment. Therefore, our educational institutions must create an atmosphere where it's acceptable for these students to demonstrate their intelligence.

Obstacles to Obtaining an Education

African-Americans are told that institutions of higher learning are places where, through hard work, they can achieve the American dream. However, due to a disproportion of finances and a lack of parental financial contributions to their education, African-American youths are forced to take out student loans in order to obtain higher education. Sure, there are governmental subsidies out there for students with financial difficulties or hardships, but it's typically not enough to pay for all of their educational expenses, especially if the student is a mediocre student.

Many people neglect to identify the role economic status plays on the decision to pursue higher education. African-American males are encouraged to pursue higher education to improve their quality of life. Yet, many have little or no family financial assistance, because they come from families that are in poverty or straddle the poverty line. Scholarships are so competitive that the odds of African-American males getting scholarships based on academic performance and a well-written scholarship essay are almost like the chances of winning the lottery. Therefore, African-American males are forced to take out student loans in order to pay rising tuition costs in pursuit of a higher education. Unfortunately, a vicious cycle is now trending with the borrowing of student loans.

After Graduation

Due to the negative stereotypes, many times African-American graduates find it difficult to find employment. The job market is so competitive they get passed over or overlooked by employers for Caucasian candidates. It's unfortunate with all their sacrifices and hard work that African-American male graduates find themselves unemployed or underemployed. African-American males are often underemployed and experience a longer period of joblessness and lower salaries in comparison to Caucasian males. Even when African-American males have higher academic credentials or more work experience, if they have education or expertise greater than the interviewers, they are passed over for employment opportunities, because interviewers are intimidated. They view the applicant or candidate as a potential threat to their job security. Many African-American male college graduates are forced to take lower paying jobs in order to make ends meet.

Meanwhile, their deferred/forbearance loan is accruing interest. Students are told that student loan debt is not looked upon negatively. However, it does show up to creditors/lenders as an outstanding debt. Unlike other loan debts, student loan debt can't be written off by filing for bankruptcy. When a student attempts to make a huge purchase, their debt-to-income ratio is assessed. If their student loan debt is astronomical and their salary/income is moderate to below average, chances are they will not be approved for a major loan, like for instance a home. Even if student loan payment arrangements have been made with the educational lender and they're placed on a payment plan they can afford, their debt-to-income ratio restricts them. Despite their years of hard work and sacrifice, it appears their financial situation is still very similar to the life of poverty they've attempted to escape.

So the question becomes, was the pursuit of education really worth the cost. In recent years, African-Americans have taken on more student loan debt than Caucasians. Some forty-two percent of African-Americans age twenty-five to fifty-five have college loans, compared to twenty-eight percent of Caucasians. This is because African-American families have less wealth. They have to borrow to go to college. Due to student loan debt, many people feel it's best to simply take their chances finding a decent paying career that doesn't require the accruing cost of higher education. At least they're not burdened with student loan debt at the end of the day.

Besides, when you compare what the college graduate is dishing out in student loan payments each month, the people without the degree may bring home more money. So the ultimate question becomes for African-American males why should they pursue a college education: for more money or for knowledge. A college degree wasn't deemed necessary in the past for African-American males, because regardless of their higher education, African-Americans were still underpaid and overlooked for certain opportunities.

Money in the Wrong Hands

During my many years of working in education, I've had to learn to face an ugly truth. It's the realization that some African-American children have been done a disservice by their parents. Strange as it may sound, there are African-American parents that would prefer their child or children be classified as "special needs" or "learning disabled." These parents deem it financially beneficial. Some parents of these alleged "special need" or "learning disabled" children rely on government or private subsidies intended to assist their children. The parents used these subsidies to cover monthly household living expenses. The parents of these children don't realize that their dependency or greed affects the child negatively psychologically and causes them to be improperly labeled throughout their education.

Then How Can We Help the Youth

Our African-American youth today are receiving several messages from mainstream media. One message our youth has received from the media is that talent is more important than education. What good is talent when you don't have the knowledge to handle personal business affairs? A lack of education is the reason why so many of our African-American athletes and entertainers find themselves bankrupt. Talent may help you to reach your dreams, but education will allow for you to continue living your dreams.

The other message is that, "you don't have to go to college to make money." They can easily get gigs on a reality television show, make a fool of themselves, and strike it rich. Many of them don't mind feeding into the negative stereotypical roles of African-Americans they're asked to portray.

"Since new developments are the products of a creative mind, we must therefore stimulate and encourage that type of mind in every way possible." (George Washington Carver)

I knew earlier in my life that my parents didn't consider college as a likely option for my future. They hadn't saved any money for me to attend college. Their vision and expectation of education didn't exceed me graduating high school. Yes, they expected and encouraged my sibling and me to get a good education and graduate high school with great grades, but they didn't see college as being necessary.

I grew up in a rural area in Georgia, and landing a blue-collar job at one of the local factories was considered success in most people's book. Prior to my own college experience, all of the stories I ever heard from my mother in regards to those that attended college were negative. I can't recall the number of stories I heard about someone's son or daughter she knew that went off to college and ended-up being kicked out of school, because they partied or drank too much alcohol. Not only had they been suspended, they were knee-deep in student loan debt, and they were now working some dead-end job.

The stories were almost enough to deter me from the college experience. However, if it had not been for my high school counselor Ms. Hazel Jackson and my Cooperative Developmental energy program (CDEP) and Mathematics Science & Engineering Academy (MSEA) coordinator Dr. Jackie Hodges, I would have surrendered to this pessimistic influence. I might not have ever realized or had an opportunity to fulfill my life's purpose. Of course, my mother never assumed her comments or actions were damaging, she assumed she was protecting me. Her misguided actions were simply the influence of the vicious cycle her parents had created about the lack of value in higher education.

Many African-American youth have grown up not being pushed to go to college, or they grow up seeing people who look like them in trades or other positions that don't require college degrees. If they don't have someone pushing them, it's easy to say higher education isn't a desirable option to them.

Earlier on, I knew that if I was going to attend college, I would have to make a way to get there on my own. The first thing I needed to do was to have the strongest academic record as possible. I worked hard to get the highest grades that I possibly could in all of my courses. When I reached high school, I took advantage of leadership opportunities in school, where I developed close relationships with teachers and administrators. I involved myself in extracurricular opportunities such as clubs and sports. I took a particular interest in football. I was a rather large teenager, so football seemed to be a natural fit. After football practice, I would work a part-time job for a few hours, just so I could have money in my pocket. My parents were having a hard enough time paying bills, so I knew they couldn't afford to give money to my brother and me to spend on our teenage desires. When I got off from work, I would spend most of the night studying in my room.

When the time came for me to start applying to potential colleges I wanted to attend, I stayed up late at night working on my college essays and personal statements. I knew I needed to present a very solid and thoughtful college applications. I made sure to apply for financial aid on time. Fortunately, my hard work paid off. I graduated at the top of my class in high school and got into a great college on an academic scholarship. Along my journey, I encountered doubters, people that told me that the road to college might prove too difficult for me. I was told that I would be competing against the brightest students around the country, and although I was considered one of the smarter students in our tiny rural hometown, I shouldn't expect too much of myself. I must admit, their remarks hurt, but I didn't let their limiting comments stop me from striving to excel and rank at the top of my collegiate class. Young African-American males must learn how to focus on their goals.

African-Americans can't expect teachers to do everything as it relates to educating their children. Parents need to stop blaming teachers for their children's failures and take responsibility for their own children. If African-American parents can put money into brand-named clothing and video games, then surely they can invest in their education. African-Americans need to start culturally enlightening their children by taking them to see landmarks and places that they learn and read about in our school system. It will make them more rounded. For those parents that can afford it, it's important that they be the first to invest in their children. Allow them to visit places that spark their imaginations. Take them to nice restaurants and hotels. Afterwards tell them to write about their experiences. Stop leaving them at home as if they are an inconvenience.

African-American students need to have the basic necessities for them to achieve success at an early age. African-American parents need to put the same passion in their children's academics as they do athletics. Parents need to sit down with them after school and help them with their studies, or find someone who can assist them if they lack the ability themselves.

Becoming Mentors in the Face of Institutional Challenges

Every successful person has had someone in their life who has provided them with love, support and disapproval. This support is often absent to those that live in at-risk communities. At-risk communities need more educators that have overcome similar conditions as the students they are teaching. Many times the teachers standing in front of African-American students can't relate to their circumstances. Therefore, students become labeled. *(Here are two examples: A young female middle-class Caucasian teacher, who has attended private school her entire life, comes from a two-parent home in the suburbs, earned her teaching degree from an Ivy league college, and gets a job working at an urban inner city high school or rural high school where the majority of the students are poverty-stricken minorities. Just the same, you have a White male teacher or coach who has lived under White privilege, telling poverty-stricken African-American boys how they should perceive their place or tackle challenges in a White male dominant world.)*

Educators have to understand the "framework" of oppression, in which dominant culture sustains power by targeting minority groups, often unconsciously. Achievement gaps cannot be adequately addressed until educators recognize their own hand in making African-American students feel unintelligent, despised, or marginalized.

Once African-American students have become labeled, they become less desirable for other educators to help them, because of their tarnished reputation. I personally think that all teachers need to visit the communities of the students in which they serve. Educators have to come to grips with their own racial issues or recall their past lives as students.

The faculty role is critical to the quality and exchange of teaching and learning. African-American males remain disproportionately underrepresented in the faculty ranks at institutions of higher education in the United States. Along with the traditional responsibilities and demands of the faculty role, African-American faculty members contend with racism, discrimination, and an anti-Black sentiment in academia, which results in race-related role strain.

Historically, Black College & Universities (HBCUs) are especially known for hiring educators with diverse ethnic background, more so than PWIs. Many African-American students attribute their decision to attend a historically Black College & University to the idea of having a "fair" college experience. Many African-American students choose HBCUs, because they want the comfort and familiar surroundings of minorities that share certain commonalities. HBCUs provide a psychologically supportive environment for African-American students. At HBCUs, African-American students don't have to prove they belong. They don't have to worry if the academic or social challenges that they face at their respective higher learning institutions are because of the color of their skin.

The perception has been that the education received from HBCUs is somehow inadequate when compared to that of PWIs. I often hear comments about HBCUs being party schools or HBCU students lacking in the area of diversity. It's disheartening that after years of producing extraordinary graduates, that we are still having the argument that HBCUs aren't as "rigorous" as some PWIs. Being a graduate of a HBCU myself, I found it highly upsetting to hear individuals say that the education received at a HBCU is inadequate when compared to PWIs. I considered myself well prepared. Once I reached graduate school, my educational level was not only comparable, but exceeded those that graduated from Ivy League PWIs across the country.

HBCUs have notable alumni who have excelled in the ranks at their respective professions and overcame enormous adversity. It is important for HBCUs to begin developing relationships with these alumni and encouraging them to be vocal about their experiences. It is important to formally track where alumni are accepted for post-graduate study and occupations. This is valuable information to show those who would try to downplay the quality of an HBCU education.

HBCUs are just as rigorous if not more demanding than PWIs. The ranking of top colleges has nothing to do with their students' academic standing. This perpetuates the belief that the education at a HBCU is below the standards of our nation's top universities, which is simply untrue. There is no true academic valuing tool or method that is being used to determine this. Furthermore, the same governing body accredits many of the HBCUs as the PWIs. So they are good enough to be accredited by the same academic standards, but the academic standards are still unequal. It's a very flawed argument at best.

HBCUs can't control their institutional narrative. They can however, attempt to provide information to the poorly informed public that attempts to diminish their students and their institutions' reputation. HBCUs contribute significantly to the African-American middle class and the nation's economy, and in spite of fewer resources, graduate in impressive numbers of majors in education, science, technology, engineering, and mathematics.

More than Capable

Many African-American males don't pursue higher education, not because they are not capable, it's because they lack knowledge about the process of obtaining degrees. African-American males hear many intimidating myths about degrees that prevent them from wanting to pursue higher education.

Many people with degrees create an idea that only a few people can obtain these higher accolades. I would dare to say that anyone with self-discipline and perseverance can obtain a higher degree, such as a master's or doctoral degree. Of course, there are those with learning disabilities that may experience more challenges. Obtaining a higher degree has nothing to do with how smart you are. It's about persistence and acquiring and utilizing the proper resources to earn the degree.

The degree itself doesn't make you better than anyone else. What you should be judged on is how you take the knowledge you've ascertained and apply it to life. Many times, people with higher degrees attempt to reinvent themselves and lose who they are. They develop a superiority complex due to their title. The problem is that people allow the accolade to become who they are, instead of allowing it to be a facet of who they are.

People with doctoral degrees are no smarter than any other person on the planet. They are simply more knowledgeable in a particular subject matter. If you desire to pursue a higher degree, then stop waiting because you're intimidated.

Many African-American males are intimidated by college, because they do not feel confident about their reading and writing skills. It's because they didn't have a strong foundation before graduating high school. If we realize that we are weak in a particular area, we need to seek out resources to improve. African-American males have to make the effort in learning what they need in order to succeed, even if it's not in the classroom. Most often, those individuals that flunk out of college do so, because they are not willing to put forth the effort to succeed. It has nothing to do with their intelligence level.

Becoming Contributing Members of the Community

Many people would argue that education is the great equalizer, more so than money. Knowledge is inevitably needed in order to improve any financial position. You have to be knowledgeable in order to obtain money. The only way to gain knowledge is through experience and education in itself. Knowledge is something no person can take away from you. People can think what they want about me, but at the end of the day they still have to refer to me with the prestigious title of doctor, because of my education.

Education has always allowed African-Americans to minutely defy the boundaries of color lines and prevail above the perceived limits of the typical Black status quo. Education is so empowering that Caucasians in the past knew that the only way to control African-Americans was to control their education. This is why reading was prohibited to African-American slaves, and during the 1950s and 1960s why the quality of education and learning resources at Black schools were second-rate to White schools.

There are over two million African-American men in the United States with a college degree, many of whom have made significant contributions in business, science, education and the arts. There should never be a lack of clarity about the contributions that African-American men have made to our country and communities.

Chapter 4:
Accepting Responsibilities

Despite historical patterns to the contrary and a slight reduction in recent years, African-American children in particular are especially likely to live in single-parent homes with their mother. In a 2008 Father's Day speech, President Obama criticized "too many" Black fathers for "abandoning their responsibilities, acting like boys instead of men." People seemed to be shock when I'm out with my wife and kids. It's disappointing that an African-American male being a good husband and father is viewed as atypical behavior. African-American males must exhibit a sense of social responsibility, as well as strong and intellectual and practical skills such as communication, analytical, and problem-solving skills.

"There are universal aspects of parenting that have been distinguished as valuable for all children, regardless of income and ethnicity. These practices include sensitive and nurturing parenting and provisions for an enriching environment. When parents are receptive and sensitive to children's needs and provide an assortment of enriching opportunities, then children's sense of independence and confidence in their skills and abilities are enhanced, strengthening their ability to deal with overcoming obstacles" (Elizabeth P. Pungello).

Gender Roles

There is a problem that plagues the African-American community. Due to the number of estranged fathers, mothers have taken on the responsibilities that fathers should be taking. Our African-American youth have seen their mothers assume these male roles and this has caused our African-American youth to devalue the presence and authority of the African-American male. In many incidents, young African-American males have assumed the role and responsibility as man of the house in single parent homes with their mothers. They are rarely inspired to leave the nest, because the household becomes dependent upon their income.

I'm a religious man. I believe the grand divine scheme of things, as it relates to gender roles, is for fathers to provide children with a sense of tough love and mothers a warm soothing position. It allows a child to develop balance. I still believe the male is the head of the household. Socially, men and women are equal, but functionally, they're different.

I commend African-American mothers that raise male children on their own. However, it's difficult for an African-American female to teach young African-American males how to be African-American men. A woman can attempt to teach a young man the traits that a responsible man should possess, but she will never truly understand the experience of his position in society. This is a lesson that only another African-American male can teach him. Young African-American males often times don't have fathers residing in the home to serve as everyday role models. Without paternal involvement, boys are more likely to develop ideas about what it means to be a man based on negative media portrayals and depictions.

Our African-American mothers have coddled and cradled young African-American males. They've been handicapped by unadulterated love and emotions. Mothers are naturally wired with feelings to protect their child from the pain of failure. However, we all know the value of a lesson learned through experience. We learn our greatest lesson when we fail; the healed scars become a reminder of how we should do things differently. Attempting to protect children from failing places them at a disadvantage in life. A mother shielding their child from taking risks essentially says that she feels that she hasn't taught the child well enough.

Mothers have a tendency of over-inflating the young African-American male's ego out of love. The mothers of these young males have lied to them. She tells him that he's great, but in truth, "he ain't there yet!" She tells him that he's special, because he's the first in the family to go to college and to get a degree among other things. It's a smart decision; yet going to college doesn't make him great or special. He's average, considering there are thousands of students being accepted into college throughout the world.

Many times when I'm speaking to these young African-American males, I tell them that, "You're not the only person in life that has been yelled at, lied to, wondered if they're loved, or to have fears. Every living breathing person in this world has or will experience and overcome tribulations. What makes each of us special is our unique level of discipline, willingness, motivation, and desire. Those that are perceived as great, will recognize, prepare, and recover sooner than others."

Mothers often times have a habit of enabling young males, using their age as an excuse to justify their persistent coddling. Their motherly instinct to nurture and protect is what ultimately leads these young African-American males to become "mama's boys." A mama's boy is a male that shies away from making a critical or rational decision without consulting their mother or can't decide. This is because the male never developed the skill to think for himself.

One of the biggest excuses I hear from mothers when their child is attempting to step out into the world and finally face challenges and assume responsibility on their own is that their child is too young. Stop using age as a handicap. Let's stop using youthfulness as today's excuse and remember most of those that played an active and vital role in the Civil Rights Movement were young African-American men and women. There was a twenty-six year old Black minister by the name of Dr. Martin Luther King that started the Civil Rights Movement. Progress seldom comes from those that are settled or secure. It comes from those who have become unsettled by what they've seen.

Parents today have a tendency to associate youthfulness with immaturity. When our young men and women refuse to follow a path or mindset many adults are accustomed to, they are often deemed as rebellious, troubled, or hard-headed. This wasn't far from the perspective of the older generation of African-Americans toward the African-American youth prior to the civil rights movement.

Although the older generation of African-Americans hated the Jim Crow era of racism and segregation, they had become complacent and accepted the injustices of that period as the norm. They felt powerless and unable to change an unfortunate circumstance that was reinforced by our government's legislative and judicial system. It took the energy, vision, and willingness of our youth of that era to stand against a flawed system of governing. So we should recognize the power our youth possess and stop crippling them with codling and our own fears. Their life's purpose may be to stand against the very same obstacles loved ones feared they might encounter.

Another issue that relates to gender roles is the limitations that are imposed by research studies that support the idea that women are more emotional than men. I consider men to be more emotional than women. African-American boys are taught not to cry as African-American men, because it supposedly shows weakness. Men have emotions that run deeper than women; men keep their feelings bottled up, internalizing more things, because they feel that they have to fulfill their gender roles as men.

Additionally, there are limitations that suggest that showing emotions is a sign of weakness. African-American men and women often display a tough or callous demeanor, because they don't want to be perceived as weak. After witnessing years of their ancestors being victimized by Caucasians, future generations of African-Americans refuse to succumb to the same fate. Therefore, any confrontational occurrences with Caucasians or any ethnic group becomes an opportunity to defy the fate their ancestors experienced. If we only rely on stereotypes and traditional gender roles, we risk not providing African-American men and women the best opportunities to live successful lives.

Male Bonding

In the African-American community, the local barbershop has always been a place where men from various walks of life could sit and discuss matters in a civilized manner. I can recall a discussion I had with a group of young African-American males. They were proudly confessing aloud to everyone that they were good fathers, because they took care of their kids financially. They were sitting there in reverence, as if they deserved a trophy, waiting to receive praises from others in regards to their actions.

Wanting them to realize their responsible role as men, I interjected and intentionally threw a proverbial rock at their egos by stating, "I'm happy that you see fit to see after YOUR OWN children, the children you helped conceive during moments of erotic pleasure. I'm happy that you consider yourself a good father young brotha, but taking care of your kids is what you're supposed to do as a man. It doesn't impress anyone that you take care of YOUR kids, because they're YOUR responsibility.

Look at it from this perspective. You don't get a check or 'Thank You' card in the mail when you pay your utility bills or mortgage. Yet, you pay them anyway, because you understand it's your responsibility. If you want to impress others, help someone else's kid. Be a father figure to a child who doesn't have a strong male role model to look up to. That's what extraordinary MEN do! Being average means that you're only going to take care of your needs. But being extraordinary means that you move beyond your own self interests."

My father's biological dad was absent in his life. In fact, he never knew him. Tragically, his mother died prior to his teenage years. His stepfather assumed the responsibility of partially raising him. His stepfather loved him and acknowledged him as his son, yet he was still somewhat absent in my father's life.

Although my father's stepfather was willing to continue the responsibility of raising him and his siblings, my father's maternal side of the family thought it would be best for their maternal grandmother to raise the children. Unfortunately, her life span was short and my father and his siblings found themselves looking for another caretaker to raise them. My father was a teenager at the time of his grandmother's death. My great aunts and uncles decided that their eldest sister would raise the children. She had children nearly the same age as my father and his siblings, so they assumed the children would adjust well.

My father had to figure out how to become a man on his own during the time he was in transition between caretakers. During the time their eldest aunt was supposed to be looking after the children, she was battling her own addiction to alcohol. She was usually in a foul mood and her attitude reflected her pain. She told my father and her middle son that they would never amount to anyone or anything.

Feeling the need to overcome his current circumstance, my father set out on his own when he became legally old enough. Along life's journey, he encountered a few good people that nurtured the virtues they saw in him. They inspired him to better his circumstances, despite the odds he had previously faced as a child. My father eventually found my mother. They married and started a life together. It wasn't long before having children made its way into the picture. My father made a vow to be present and accounted for in the lives of his own children after reflecting back on his own childhood without a strong male figure present. However, just because my father was in my life doesn't mean I didn't have hurdles to cross on my own. Having my father around simply made my burdens easier to bear.

Life is About Choices

If anyone really wants to improve their situation, they should always work on the one thing they have control over—themselves. Stop blaming others for our children's shortcomings. Shame often causes us to view ourselves as victims. Consequently, whether we blame others or condemn ourselves for our actions, we sink into the depths of feeling sorry for ourselves. African-American males need to possess the capacity to perceive and address problems affecting their communities. They must make warranted judgments and act while continuously engaging themselves in lifelong learning.

Stop using God's supposed will as a cop-out for your own poor choices. *"One of the most important things that I have learned…is that life is all about choices. On every journey you take, you face choices. At every fork in the road, you make a choice. And it is those decisions that shape our lives." (Mike DeWine)* Some of us refuse to invest any part of ourselves in responsible roles. Many times we use the excuse 'we don't know.' It's because we fail to ask, or we lack the knowledge to know what we should ask. We justify not knowing, because we mistakenly believe it excuses our accountability.

"Ninety-nine percent of the failures come from people who have the habit of making excuses." (George Washington Carver)

Chapter 5:
Together we stand, "My Brother's Keeper"

America's history, democracy, economy and social infrastructure are undeniably stronger today because of the contributions of Black males past and present in their roles as sons, fathers, husbands, inventors, businessmen, doctors, lawyers, philanthropists, and veterans. As a result of enduring negative stereotypes, young African-American males today are deceived into believing that the negative stereotypes represent who they really are and who they should strive to become. African-Americans are the only race that feed into the negative imagery of themselves. It's upsetting to hear Blacks refer to themselves as a Gangster, Hustlers, Thug, or Pimp. These are not individuals African-Americans should idolize or glorify.

Glorifying Poverty

African-Americans need to stop glorifying poverty as if it's validation for how Black they are. If you listen to the interviews from African-American musicians, athletes, and actors, you would swear one criterion for being Black is being raised in subsidized housing projects, a.k.a. "The Hood" or "Ghetto." The media portrays that all African-Americans come from broken homes, poor families, or live in the hood. If these African-Americans are so proud of the hood, ask yourself, why do they leave the hood when they become successful? A better question would be, why don't they invest in those individuals in the hood, so they too might make it out of poverty? I get tired of hearing the overly publicized success story of the African-American male from the ghetto or hood, becoming successful through sports or music and now he's the role model for Black kids around the world. In comparison, other ethnic groups encourage the doctors, lawyers, politicians, and business leaders to serve as role models to their children.

Role Models Bringing Back to the Communities They Serve

I think we're all looking for a role model, someone to inspire us. A role model or an idol is a person who at the end of the day has their own hurdles they have to overcome. Be careful when attempting to find role models. Role models can be self-limiting to a person, because we feel that whatever it is we want to do must have already been done. We must be the type of person to follow our own heart and start our own dream, whether we have a role model(s) or not.

Successful African-American males that came out of poverty need to revisit their former at-risk community. *"The task ahead of us is never as great as the power behind us." (Ralph Waldo Emerson)* Our African-American young men need to see that it is possible for them to become successful in spite of their circumstances. It seems that the problem is that our young African-American males often times can't identify with success outside the confines of their neighborhood drug dealer or what's on television. With the media outlets parading young African-American males signing million dollar sports and music contracts, and the frequency with which they show movies and videos with African-Americans in expensive cars and houses, you'd think a larger percentage of the African-American population was rich. The media continuously bombards our televisions, radios, magazines, and the Internet with images of fancy cars, expensive clothes, beautiful women, and enormous multi-million dollar homes. This, in conjunction with the drug dealer, rappers, and athletes' lifestyles, all portray the same image, so many of them will mimic the behavior of those they perceive as successful.

The dangers escalate as African-American males become adolescents. Like most teenagers, they battle raging hormones and identity crises. Many rebels try to fit in by mimicking those around them or what they see on television. Unfortunately, when they make mistakes, they succumb to the full wrath of our judicial system. They are viewed as a menace to society. Young African-American males are seen as older and less innocent when compared to their Caucasian male peers. When Caucasian police officers see Caucasian teenagers, they're reminded of their own children, nieces or nephews acting out for attention, so they give them a slap on the wrist. Whereas when young African-American teenagers make the same mistakes, they are rarely granted leniency.

It almost seems as if our judiciary system is designed to protect the assets and interests of rich Caucasians and keep other colors and social classes in their respective lanes. A clear example of this would be in the case of the sentencing of a sixteen-year old White male teen from Fort Worth, Texas that received national attention.

In this particular case, the ruling judge sentenced the sixteen-year old teen that killed four people in a drunk-driving crash to ten years of probation and to attend a rehabilitation facility paid for by his parents. At the time of the accident, the White teen had seven passengers riding in his truck. His blood-alcohol level was three times that of the legal limit for an adult. The teen also had traces of Valium in his system when he lost control of his pickup truck and ran into a group of people helping a woman whose car had stalled.

Prior to sentencing, a psychologist called by the defense, testified that the White teen was a product of "affluenza." The psychologist argued that the White teen's family felt that wealth bought privilege and there was no rational link between behavior and consequences. The psychologist used the example that the teen's parents gave no punishment after police ticketed the then fifteen-year-old when he was found in a parked pickup with a passed out, undressed, fourteen-year old girl.

He continued that instead of prison, the teen was emotionally flat and needed years of therapy.

Given the "affluenza" defense—along with the fact that the teen's parents would be the ones paying for his stay at a $450,000-a-year, in-patient rehabilitation facility—this incident is one clear example of the double standards of our judiciary system. This ruling would have never been given to an African-American teen that might be considered too poor to supposedly know right from wrong.

The negative stereotypes associated with African-American males make them targets to police brutality or excessive force. It's human nature to have a preconceived opinion about others. Some wouldn't admit or go as far as to call it prejudice, but in truth, that's exactly what it is. When you have an opinion about any person or group before you meet them, and your perception of them is based off of notions from outside influences or sources like the media or someone else's opinion, that's prejudice; you've pre-judged them. Police officers aren't excluded from this truth.

If a police officer allows himself or herself to feed into the negative stereotypes about African-American males, they will automatically perceive them as a threat, even when the criminal infraction is as minor as a traffic violation. If the police officer is not properly trained, then they're more inclined to react off of impulse and fear, rather than adhere to proper training protocol. When this happens, any gesture exhibited by the African-American (a slight arbitrary movement of the hand or conduct of anger/ irritation/ aggravation) is perceived as dangerous, which causes the police officer to justify the use of excessive force or discharge their firearm.

Once African-American males are incarcerated for one crime, they will always be treated poorly and be discriminated against, because of that single act, or even because of the fact they went to jail. When these young Black males are released from prison, their lives are transformed forever. They are looked down upon for what they allegedly did, even if they've worked relentlessly to change their circumstances. In meeting with people who have been branded criminals or felons at an early age, they are denied basic civil and human rights for life and treated as though their lives don't matter.

If we are going to address and determine that these lives matter, as we should, then we need to face the difficult fact that good African-American men are not stepping up to the plate as role models. African-American neighborhood ministers reach only a small audience. The good fathers, uncles, and cousins are seen only by a few. Therefore, these positive influences do not reach the masses. Instead, their influence is localized and does not have far-reaching effects. In addition to these obvious inequalities, we must also look at who the role models for young African-American males are in today's society. The neighborhood drug dealer often becomes an idol to young African-American males and females, because they are the closest thing in reality to what they view on television as it relates to celebrities that they deem successful.

It's the drug dealers that didn't go to college who are the most popular and who are feared. Fear equals respect in many of their minds. These are the same individuals in the neighborhood that they see with rolls of money, the brand-named clothing, multiple fancy cars, the expensive jewelry, VIP treatment or access to the hottest clubs and parties, popping bottles in the club, making it rain money, and beautiful followers. It becomes difficult for the average Joe, with a high school diploma or a college degree, working nine-to-five and barely making above minimum wage, to tell them that the drug dealer lifestyle is not the direction they should follow.

If You Don't Then Here's What Happens

Based upon the role models provided by the media, and stereotypical images that run rampant in the Black communities, the successful African-American is an athlete or entertainer. African-American athletes, in particular,

90

continue to be admired and paid for their size, strength, and agility. In other words, Black men today are finding financial reward and public validity for fulfilling the same physical tasks as their enslaved ancestors. The stereotype that has emerged is the only way an African-American can become financially well off or make it out of poverty is to excel in sports or entertainment. Therefore, we see African-American parents putting more emphasis on athleticism, rapping, and singing, rather than investing into their child's academics. Like so many other young African-American males, no one realistically ever told me that becoming a doctor, lawyer, or corporate businessman was possible.

The media provides us with images of wealthy athletes, who neither focus nor mention their education outside of the college they attended; you don't know if they necessarily graduated. It seems to be the dream of most African-American athletes to play at the Division I level. This is considered the highest level of intercollegiate athletics sanctioned by the National Collegiate Athletic Association (NCAA) in the United States.

These schools are the major collegiate athletic powers, with larger budgets, more elaborate facilities, and more athletic scholarships. To get an athletic scholarship is indeed an honor that an athlete should be proud to obtain. However, it amazes me that colleges still admit student athletes with GPA and SAT/ACT scores significantly lower than what is required as their minimum standard for other applying students. It appears the message these institutions of higher learning are sending out is that your education level can be below average if you're good at sports and are able to help the college make money by putting fans in seats.

What concerns me is the number of African-American male college athletes that play at the Division I level who fail to obtain a degree. Or worse, they major in disciplines where their degree does not present them with employment opportunities after graduation. It seems that many of these athletes place all of their hopes and energy into aiming to make it to the pro-level of competition, yet they fail to take advantage of their educational opportunities. The question remains:

what happens to these athletes if they don't make it to the pros? Has the college/university experience provided them with the education and resources they need to be marketable in their search for employment opportunities?

The NFL, NBA, and the Entertainment profession have changed the trajectory of young African-American males to the point where they seem to think the only way to gain success is through sports. These organizations endorse the "get rich quick mentality." The "get rich quick" mentality has had much to do with the African-American high school dropout rate and why young African-American males find themselves in our penitentiaries after breaking the law. It's because the Black community seems to worship those that have gotten rich quickly.

Americans have become infatuated by those with money. This explains why Americans tune in nightly on their televisions to watch rich celebrities enjoy the high life. The story of real life has been distorted. In many incidences, the lives of the celebrities we're watching are far from the glitz and glamor the camera portrays. The fancy houses, luxurious cars, and the expensive toys are all rented or leased. It's the American dream the media is attempting to sell to the public. What African-Americans have to understand is that most of their children will not get rich quickly. With each presentation of an athlete's million-dollar-a-year contract, or Oprah's status as an African-American billionaire, a shroud of deception is created within the overall American economic psyche about the immense Black wealth disparity. Young Black men across America that used to dream of making great changes in racial inequity, now just dream of being a millionaire through athletics or entertainment. (Antonio Moore – Huffington Post 2014)

Despite a large section of African-American households drowning in poverty and debt, the stories of a few are told as if they represent the majority. As African-American celebrities welcome viewers into their homes through various television shows, and the news advertises another young Black athlete signing a multi-million dollar contract, Americans seem to forget the overall disproportion of financial affairs.

Language barriers

The use of proper grammar is not reinforced often in African-American homes. African-Americans have been said to butcher the English language. The communication styles in today's world are so vast in difference that it sets barriers in communication. The impacts are so complex that it makes communicating between cultures difficult.

Cultural and language differences can hinder effective communication. Language is the key to a person's self-identity. Language can have a significant impact on the quality of our interactions. It enables the person to express emotions, share feelings, and convey knowledge. Language is our greatest mediator that allows us to relate and understand each other. Many times we are unaware of how language impacts our lives, our relationships, and our careers.

When African-Americans speak well, they are often times ridiculed by other Blacks for "talking White." This statement implies that Caucasians inherently speak or communicate better than African-Americans. Communication, which is a two-way process, is a learned skill and takes practice. There are African-Americans that refuse to improve their communication skills because they fear that it makes them somehow less "Black." When African-Americans refuse to improve communication skills, the decision becomes another means by which employers can rationalize covert racial employment discrimination. They are able to justify not hiring the African-American candidate by stating they possess a "language barrier."

Understanding the Lingo

I've noticed that the expression, ***"You feel me?"*** is commonly used amongst African-Americans when communicating with each other. I realize that this phrase denotes that African-Americans subconsciously recognize that there is an inherited force that connects them to each other. This force allows for African-

Americans to share each other's experiences through mere dialogue. The expression has a deeper, almost spiritual meaning. Like I see into you, I understand you, and I acknowledge your emotions and spirit.

It's the African-American spirit that allows them to use the phrase in appropriate contexts and with proper intonation. ***"You feel me?"*** is associated with gaining an accurate comprehension of another African-American. It's about perceiving the true nature of reality beneath surface appearances. It's African-Americans' ability to empathize with each other that gives them this ability to perceive and experience the world from each other's perspective—feeling *with* rather than feeling *for*.

Mental Health

While the African-American experience in the United States is rampant with incidents of subjugation and displacement, it is also characterized by amazing individual and collective strengths that have enabled many African-Americans to survive and do well, often against enormous adversity. African-Americans, who've climbed the socio-economic and professional hierarchy in the face of institutionalized racism, struggle with feeling compelled to be strong. Some are so socially remote that they feel they can't trust anyone or share anything and must go at it alone. African-American males are very private, so it makes it difficult for others to help them. It's an inherent defense mechanism learned and passed down from their ancestors during slavery.

During slavery, the slave masters planted seeds of distrust amongst the African-American slaves so that they would not confide in each other and rise up against them. The residual effects of those seeds can still be seen. African-Americans keep pressing matters a secret and bottle up their emotional issues/pain. Even when problems are evident and are taking a strain on their lives, they refuse to accept or identify that there is a problem. These bound-up emotions have led to the mental health issues that African-Africans refuse to acknowledge and get help for today.

During slavery, mental illness often resulted in a more inhumane existence including frequent beatings and abuse, which forced many slaves to hide their issues. The reason why there aren't more mental health stories in the African-American community is because the topic is viewed as taboo. African-Africans are less inclined to seek help for mental health issue when they don't see anybody else that looks like them talking about their challenges.

The Limits of Trust

"United States of America, when it came to treating her citizens of Indian descent fairly, she failed. She put them on reservations. When it came to treating her citizens of Japanese descent fairly, she failed. She put them in internment prison camps. When it came to treating her citizens of African descent fairly, America failed. The government put them in chains. She put them on slave quarters, put them on auction blocks, put them in cotton fields, put them in inferior schools, put them in sub-standard housing, put them in scientific experiments, put them in the lowest paying jobs, put them outside the equal protection of the law, kept them out of their racist bastions of higher education, and locked them into positions of hopelessness and helplessness. The government gives them the drugs, builds bigger prisons, passes a three strike law, and then wants us to sing God Bless America." (Rev. Jeremiah Wright)

The difference between African-Americans and other ethnic groups is that after America failed and persecuted their race, they realize how much they needed to stick together and empower each other. As soon as African-Americans broke the shackles of segregation, and tasted a piece of equality, they started to focus their attention on White affirmation. Despite their ancestors' history of deceit and conquest of civilizations around the globe, the general consensus is that most of the world still sees Caucasians as trustworthy, reliable, and honest.

When a Caucasian person interacts with an African-American, they may not realize that while their skin color is often an asset, when interacting with African-Americans it may be counted against them. It's their whiteness itself that often provokes mistrust. At least initially, until they prove themselves.

Just as Caucasians tend to size up new African-American individuals in racial terms, waiting for the Black person to prove him or herself better than the "negative Black stereotype," African-Americans often do the same thing to Caucasian people. For African-Americans, Caucasians must prove that they're not going to exhibit negative stereotypical White tendencies before they can be trusted.

I sometimes hear Caucasians complain about being treated differently by African-Americans, differently from what looks like the more friendly ways that African-Americans treat each other. "What did I do to deserve such cold treatment?" Caucasians sometimes say.

In most cases, African-Americans hold a degree of distrust of Caucasians. This is because African-Americans tend to know more about Caucasians than Caucasians do about African-Americans. Think about it. In our public school systems, students (including African-American students) spend years learning about European culture and American history. History is often times biased and told from the perspective of those in power. Therefore, American history is told from the perspective of Caucasians. Students spend very little time, if any, learning about Black culture or any other race's culture.

America's education system has failed to present accurate African-American history in schools. African-Americans have primarily been depicted in subordinate roles and more or less sub-human. When these history texts refer to the African culture, they use derogatory statements relating to primitive heathenish qualities of the African background. They neglect to mention the skills, abilities, and contributions of Blacks to mankind's existence. The disregard of African-

American history and distortion of the events concerning Blacks in most history texts, deprive Black children of their racial heritage, and relegated them to nobody or nothing. Lack of knowledge about their prevailing heritage, ultimately drain Black youths of their self-confidence, self-respect, and self-knowledge.

It's obvious when Caucasians have had little exposure to African-Americans. They are overly polite and unsure of how to interact. Likewise, African-Americans are guarded or distant, remembering lessons learned from other African-Americans' pain: keep Caucasians at arm's length and out of their personal business. What Caucasians should recognize and somehow tell each other, is that when African-Americans seem guarded, standoffish, or even rude, it may be because they don't trust them. It's up to the Caucasian to show that they can be trusted, which can take time.

Caucasians seldom know what African-Americans really think or feel about things. African-Americans and Caucasians don't talk together much about racial issues, and even when they do, the issue of racial trust never comes up. While I'm a very friendly and personable person, most of my relatives often keep Caucasians at arm's length. Maybe the most painful thing about being able to see through the overly polite performance of a covert racist Caucasian is that it can be incredibly alienating when the African-American feels that they're the only one who is aware that such an act is being performed, that someone is being condescending and duplicitous to them because of their race.

African-Americans have always harbored a sense of distrust and lack of faith in our judiciary and legislative systems in America. Who can blame them, especially when you look at incidents like:

- Innocent African-Americans being judged guilty by an alleged group of their peers: biased all White juries.

- White law enforcement officers safeguarding the rights and interests of fellow Caucasians while leaving African-American victimized.

- Being Constitutionally permitted to vote since 1869 by the Fifteenth Amendment, but systematically deprived that right by white supremacist state governments. Between 1882 and 1968, more Black people were lynched in Mississippi than in any other state. Theodore Bilbo, a Mississippi senator and a proud Klansman once stated to his fellow Caucasian constituents, "You and I know what's the best way to keep the nigger from voting. You do it the night before the election."

- African-Americans were cheated out of fair wages and paid considerably less to perform the same jobs as Caucasian employees.

- Reparations rescinded: Promissory titles to land given by the federal government granting 40 acres on which Black families could build after the Civil War were retracted, leaving them landless, homeless and jobless. In 2001, the Associated Press published a three-part investigation into the theft of Black-owned land stretching back to the antebellum period. The series documented some 406 victims and 24,000 acres of land valued at tens of millions of dollars. The land was taken through means ranging from legal chicanery to terrorism. Some of the land taken from African-American families became country clubs, oil fields, and baseball spring training facilities.

- New York City Draft Riot (1863), Atlanta Race Riot (1906), The East St. Louis Massacre (1917), Washington, D.C. Race Riots (1919), Knoxville, Tennessee Race Riots (1919), Chicago Race Riots (1919).

- Greenwood, Tulsa, Oklahoma "Black Wall Street" (May 31 – June 1, 1921).

- Rosewood Massacre (1923).

- The Tuskegee Syphilis Experiment (1932 - 1972).

- Harsher federal and state sentencing laws to target African-American male defendants in an effort to promote their mass incarceration.

Although these historic examples have given African-Americans just reasons for their distrust, African-Americans must realize that all groups are composed of individuals. Just because we may have encountered one person or a few people from a race that proved themselves to be untrustworthy, doesn't mean that everyone from that race has the same devious intentions.

Self-made Man

We have a misunderstanding that being a man and independent means not asking anyone for help. I heard young African-Americans say often, "I'm a real man. I don't want or need anyone's help, because I want to stand on my own two feet." I feel this statement is preposterous. I've seen Caucasians hired in positions simply because they were friends or relatives of employers. I've seen Caucasians placed in leadership positions, because their relatives or a friend of the family had political or financial influence. I've seen people apply for employment advancement positions where they were qualified or overly qualified and passed over, simply because the interviewer(s) decided to hire someone they already favored or shared a previous relationship. In many incidents, this individual was less qualified. Not only did this less qualified person become the other person's immediate supervisor, but also the employers instructed the subordinate to train their new supervisor.

African-American males need to realize that no one gets to a position of success without help. Any person that has had anything good happen to them has had someone put in a good word for them or get them into a position. Other ethnic groups are able to get ahead, because they utilize the resources of their relatives, friends, or social affiliations. They're not afraid to reach out and confess to others that they need help. Asking for help or asking for insight or advice doesn't mean you're less of a man or weak.

African-American males desire others to see their accomplishments as equivalent to those that are in authority. They are misled into thinking that there is a sense of nobility in the struggle for success. They presume that receiving help is unfair and others will devalue the merit of their success. Yet, African-Americans must realize that fair doesn't necessarily mean giving everyone the same thing. It's giving those that lack certain things what they need, or what you think they need, to have the same opportunities as everyone else.

How can we expect other races to respect and see us differently if we continue to devalue ourselves? African-Americans should hold themselves to the same standards as they expect other ethnic groups to adhere. That means African-Americans shouldn't refer to themselves with derogatory connotations such as niggers, regardless of how it's spelled. The origin of the term is still the same. The word "nigger" is not a person it's a personality. This also means we shouldn't use derogatory terms like this to describe other races. African-Americans must have a sense of humility.

Representing Our Communities

It is said that no one man can exemplify an entire race of people. However, each day, every personal encounter a Black male has with those outside his race creates the standard by which every other African-American male will be perceived. Therefore, the legacy of one becomes the legacy of the whole.

I think Black non-Americans often distance themselves from the African-American experience and from being "seen" as Black American, because of the negative image and pain that may be associated with the Black experience in the United States. Every African I have ever met, made sure to go out of their way to make sure others knew that they were not Black Americans. Consequently, I've always presumed this was a way to indicate their ancestors never experienced the indignity of slavery; they weren't tainted by the whip and chain.

"If we have the courage and tenacity of our forebears, who stood firmly like a rock against the lash of slavery, we shall find a way to do for our day what they did for theirs." (Mary McLeod Bethune)

We all know who and what the problems are in our communities. Yet, we turn a blind eye until it affects our lives. If you're not part of the solution, then you're part of the problem. A long habit of tolerating something wrong gives the superficial appearance of it being okay. I think African-Americans take for granted what their ancestors died and fought for. What would they say about them: not voting, calling each other derogatory names, and killing each other? I'm sure this is not the legacy they wanted to leave behind.

Still today, whenever there's racial tension, African-Americans have a habit of rioting, destroying and ransacking their own communities. This act makes no sense. Those Caucasians in power laugh, because they could care less.

We are accountable for holding others accountable. The media uses distractions to take our minds off of key issues and policies that affect our communities. I'm saddened every time I drive down a street named after Dr. Martin Luther King Jr. throughout the US. I've noticed a sad correlation. It seems that streets named after MLK are in predominately African-American neighborhoods where the homes are poorly maintained and the crime rate is disturbingly high. African-Americans are partly to blame, as are the elected city officials that represent those communities. It appears that across America maintaining the infrastructure of African-American neighborhoods is not set as a high priority in comparison to predominantly Caucasian neighborhoods.

Life is political, and many African-Americans lack strong political relationships with those in leadership. If race wasn't considered an important factor in the United States and how we govern, then ask yourself, why do politicians and political parties spend so much time and money devising ways to appeal to the various ethnic groups for campaign purposes? African-Americans need to stop letting politicians victimize them. Believing that African-Americans need mass assistance or initiatives suggests that African-Americans are inherently less capable than other races. I would argue that the politicians African-Americans help elect can't relate to their issues. Sure, they paint the picture that they're the average Joe, but most of them are far from average.

I'm sure you've noticed that the individuals elected to political offices are typically from wealthy Caucasian families. Every once in a while, the average African-American Joe gets elected, but he or she will have to quickly pick a side or their political career will be short-lived. So it appears that change many times doesn't happen in African-American communities, because the interests of the politicians they elect never seem to coincide with the interests of the people.

I've noticed that the people we often elect for political offices are relatives of those already or formerly voted to political positions. Since they are related it makes sense to assume that they have the same values, especially if their relatives are the individuals endorsing their campaign. That doesn't imply that everyone from these family trees are full of rotten apples, but they may cultivate relationships and connections that can help siblings, cousins, and in-laws win elections.

A study found that Congress members who serve more than one term have a forty percent chance of someone in their family later ending up in Congress. American politics has become another type of family business. It's difficult for change to occur, because many of the officials we elect to office are what I refer to as legacy candidates. These are individuals that are members of political families or "dynasties" such as: the Adam Family, Bush Family, Clinton Family, Daley Family, Frelinghuysen Family, Harrison Family, Kennedy Family, Lee Family, Long Family, Muhlenberg Family, Rockefeller Family, Roosevelt Family, Taft Family, or Udall Family. These are families that have political influence at a national level, but think about all the local political families in your town.

It appears for most African-Americans, the only time they ever see their elected officials is during campaign time. Not all politicians have their own interests at heart, but many politicians' loyalties often lie with those individuals or companies contributing financially to their campaign. This is political influence not afforded to those living in poverty. They feel as if they don't possess any power or political influence. This rationalization contributes to why people in poverty-stricken areas are reluctant to vote.

A Multicultural Life – Defying Stereotypes

African-Americans must learn to work with people that are good people, not because they look like them. Many times it's the people we assume or expect to help us, that will ultimately stand in our way. Sometimes, it's just the opposite; the person we least expect to help us might be the person to aid us when we need help the most. We need to remove labels we've placed on individuals, because of their age, color, occupation, education, or religion. African-Americans are often times as judgmental as those we condemn; we must be careful not to be hypocritical. Realize that everyone is on top at some point in his or her life.

The topic takes my mind back to a story that one of my clients shared in regards to not judging a person by their color, but rather by their character.

There was a homeless African-American man that used to loiter a block away from a comedy club in Chicago, Illinois. He was once a powerful attorney until his wife and kids died in a fatal car crash. He was so devastated by the incident he fell into a state of depression. He started to drink heavily and literally lost everything. He had stopped drinking, but he found it difficult to get back on his feet. It was the month of October and the nights had started to get cold.

There were four men that crossed his path. As he was standing motionless in the corner of one of the buildings attempting to shield himself from the freezing wind, he called out to the first African-American that crossed his path. The gentleman must have been on a date, because he was dressed fairly nicely and was accompanied by a female who also was dressed well. He approached the couple as they stood next to a Caucasian couple also waiting to cross the street.

Turning his back towards the Caucasian couple and directing his attention toward the African-American couple, he said, "Excuse me my brotha and sistha, I hate to bother you good folks, but by chance would you have a spare coat anywhere you wouldn't mind giving me? It's extremely cold and I fear that I might not make it on the streets this winter without one."

The African-American couple looked at him in disgust. The woman resumed to clutch her purse tightly and moved behind her companion as if he were a shield. The woman stated that she had already done all the good deeds she intended to for the year and that they were not a homeless shelter. Her African-American male companion went as far as to curse the homeless man and told him to find a shower and a job. Disappointed and insulted, the homeless man held his head down and walked back over to the corner where he had initially been standing.

A few moments later, another African-American gentlemen crossed his path. The homeless man asked, "Brotha, do you have a spare coat I might use."

The gentleman stated that he was in a rush to get home, but he would return a bit later to bring him one of his old jackets. The homeless man smiled and told the gentleman, "Thank you." The homeless man waited for hours patiently, until it was obvious that the gentleman had no intentions of returning. About an hour later, another African-American gentleman on his cellphone walked by.

The homeless man endeavored desperately to get the African-American gentleman's attention, "Sir! Sir! Excuse me sir!"

Yet the gentleman pretended that he didn't exist. He just kept walking as if the homeless man hadn't spoken a word to him. After hours had passed without success, the realization came upon the homeless man that he might never find a coat to stay warm through the harsh approaching winter. As the homeless man began to gather his belongings and place them into an old rusty shopping cart, a Caucasian man approached him. It was the same Caucasian man he had turned his back on earlier.

The Caucasian gentleman stated, "My wife and I walked a few blocks to get you a cup of coffee."

The Caucasian man stated, "Brother you look cold." Unexpectedly, he began to remove his coat and gave it to the homeless man.

The homeless man examined the coat carefully. He could tell that it was very expensive. The Caucasian man smiled and said, "I know you don't consider me your brother, but we're all one big family in the creator's eyes, so I consider you my brother." The homeless man nodded his head, exemplifying that he had just become enlightened.

Years later, the homeless man had gotten back on his feet and had made a name for himself once again. Much to his surprise, while riding in his limo, he saw the Caucasian man that had helped him years ago, now homeless on the streets just as he had been. He shouted to his driver, "Stop the car!"

He got out of the limo and approached the man. He said, "I never forget a face. It was you that helped me years ago when I was cold and homeless. I still have the coffee cup and coat you gave me that October night. I keep them in a glass case in my mansion to remind me that help often times comes from the people you least expect. With that being said sir, allow me to help you brotha'."

We shouldn't assume that because a person shares our ethnicity or color that they desire to see us succeed. We should accept people, because they are "good people," not because they look like us. I've had more Caucasians contribute to my personal success thus far than African-Americans. African-Americans frequently place the sole blame on Caucasians for the captivity of countless of their Black ancestors. Yet, African-Americans forget it was fellow Africans who first enslaved each other. African-Americans attempt to portray Africa as a utopia before Caucasians sailed over and enslaved their race. Please don't be naive.

There's a difference between "Ideal Africa" and "Real Africa." When many African-Americans visit Africa for the first time, they go expecting the paradise of "Ideal Africa." When they're confronted by "Real Africa," they realized that even Blacks for their homeland *(with very little Caucasian exposure or influence)* are capable of the same iniquities as any other race of people.

Not every Caucasian has a vendetta against African-Americans, nor does every African-American have their best interest at heart. There were Caucasians fighting and dying beside African-Americans to gain freedoms. Therefore, African-Americans must never forget that they didn't reach freedom on their own. African-Americans should have no time to hate any one. All their time should be devoted to the up-building and development of the African-American race.

Staying True to Yourself and Learning about Your Heritage

I was conversing with a "self-proclaimed" African-American civil rights leader about the African-American diaspora. In the midst of our conversation, he stated, "I don't see how anyone would want to visit, much less live in Africa." His statement astounded me. His statement bothered me, because it shows how far African-Americans are removed from their ancestral homeland. In fact, they are so far displaced that they now fear it. The mainstream media bombards Americans with images of African savagery, famine, and disease. Then we form our opinions of how lucky African-Americans are, because they have been removed from those alleged terrible conditions. We don't realize that the depicted images are intended to provoke these feelings.

Chapter 6:
Hazardous Working Environments

I often ask myself, "Why are Blacks so rare at the highest echelons of leadership. African-Americans feel honored when they have been chosen to represent their race in leadership roles. Other times, they see it as a burden, because they feel that they have to be someone other than who they really are for 8 to 12 hours a day. While everyone needs to create and put forth an appropriate workplace identity, this becomes particularly true for African-Americans, because their working identities must counter common cultural and negative racial stereotypes. The attributes of African-American leadership that Caucasian Americans prefer in Blacks in authority positions are: those with modest haircuts/hairstyles; slender body frames; come from a nuclear family structure; and reside in a predominantly Caucasian neighborhood. African-American leadership can be visibly Black, but at the same time, they don't want to be perceived as stereotypically Black.

Companies that employ more sensitive company leaders or executives and that respond to increased social pressures usually appoint Blacks into leadership positions. In the absence of these institutional pressures, companies would ignore putting Blacks into leadership roles. Employers search for African-American leaders who make them comfortable. Some companies seem to be satisfied after hiring one or two Blacks, and do little afterwards to enhance diversity. Their employers groom most Caucasian males for years to become leaders at their place of employment. African-American males typically have to leave their place of employment for growth opportunities or move around the company to find someone who is currently in a leadership role willing to give them an opportunity to prove themselves. Unconscious biases against people who don't look like a "typical" (a.k.a. White male) leader can make it harder for African-American leaders to climb the company ladder. Some companies haven't quite figured out how to effectively recruit, cultivate, and retain African-American talent.

Leaders are often subconsciously more comfortable working with people like themselves. People have a tendency to select individuals that they are familiar with and comfortable with, noting that a vast majority of board members and leaders in companies are still Caucasian males. Since they are more comfortable with their network, the people that get those opportunities tend to look like them.

When Blacks soar to leadership roles such as CEO, President, Supervisor, Manager, Director, or Team leader, it gives other Blacks a glimmer of hope and pride. Most Blacks consider it an honor to have one of their own calling the shots in their place of employment for a change. When you look at the African-American legacy of being victims of racism and discrimination, it brings a smile to your face to see how far your race has come. Their Black leader's success of overcoming racial barriers is felt as a racial triumph for all Blacks working at that establishment.

However, having more African-American leaders or coworkers isn't a guarantee of better working conditions. Although Black subordinates are often times happy with their respective Black leader's accomplishment, they are discontent with their leadership. The question I'm concerned with is why? I was saddened to discover that Blacks in leadership roles have a tendency to ignore racial issues affecting Black subordinates. Yet, Black leadership often conforms, or attempts to fit in, with White colleagues that hold similar or higher positions. Black leaders have proved unwilling or unable to defend the very institutional policies that made their own emergence to the top of their respective organizations possible. It seems Blacks in leadership compromise their racial integrity to fit into their position. Many times, they seem so far removed from racial and discriminatory matters that Black subordinates wonder if they care. Black subordinates expect their Black leaders to share racial empathy.

Many Black leaders attempt to justify their neglect in addressing racial issues concerning Black and White employees by saying "they can't appear to show racial favoritism," even when it's clear that Whites are the antagonists in the matter. Black leaders attempt to convince black subordinates that question their blind eye that they lack an understanding of the full dimension of the nature of their position to the status quo forces. The status quo represents the Caucasians that place them in their position. It's very common for Whites to choose Black leaders that will sway in favor of the status quo when dealing with matters that affect their subordinates.

Black leaders have proven that they are powerless in preventing inequality in their organization. Black leaders must dare to impart impolite and unpleasant truths to the powerful and the well-connected. When Black subordinates sympathize with ineffective closemouthed Black leaders, they undermine any company policies that aim to effectively pressure Black leadership into reprimanding racial or discriminatory practices. Black people are trapped in a vicious cycle of looking at their Black leader and revering them, yet their Black leader is not willing to acknowledge that he is racially aligned with the subordinates and should represent the minority.

While African-Americans are struggling to fit in with their Caucasian colleagues, some are also faced with a disconnect between themselves and the other African-Americans who are less professionally accomplished in their work environment. Black leaders often pose the rhetorical question, "Why is my Blackness considered too much for Whites and not enough for Blacks?" The odds are very much against them. In all their smarts and their fancy suits, they will still be perceived as the Token Black person, or the "Sellout."

Even if an African-American is being tokenized as the only Black person in leadership, they're still expected to conform to the Caucasian perspectives. Tokenizing means to hire one person of a certain race with the expectation that they will represent everyone from that race. There is a psychological and interpersonal pressure from being any organization's "Token Black." Being the "Token Black" comes with knowing that your every move, every misstep, every blunder will be used to judge everyone like you. Often employers come right out and ask African-American employees to speak for all Black people.

People navigate the world around them with their stereotypes of others. Of course, nobody leaves that stereotype at home just because they're heading off to work. Even in their leadership roles, African-Americans tend to be "skating on thin ice" and have less freedom to lead than their Caucasian counterparts. They are always under the microscope, because they don't look like the stereotypical model of a leader. Whites will still think of them as sub-par. They'll think them unreliable. They'll think them belligerent. They'll think them lazy. They'll think that he or she doesn't belong in the leadership position. If these African-American leaders fail in their role, a Caucasian will replace them, most of the time.

Racism in the Work Environment

Most African-Americans have heard the story of the Black person with a degree who got passed over for a promotion that was given to a Caucasian, who barely had a GED. Most African-Americans would rather own their own business, because they don't want to tolerate the humiliation of attempting to "fit" into the status quo. Yet, most Blacks don't have the money to start a serious business even if they have a great idea. African-Americans are often put into uncomfortable positions in predominately White working environments. They often find themselves overlooking racist comments or jokes, instead of admitting that it hurt them. All in an attempt to avoid being labeled the "Angry Black person" at work. African-American employees' experiences often also include having to hide the struggle of dealing with race when they're at work.

African-Americans are often expected to carry the burden of racism silently, because when they talk about it, they're seen as causing problems. Many African-Americans are familiar with this cycle: they witness or experience racism; point it out or stand up for themselves; and then the Caucasian cries, or feels guilty, or says they're being attacked. Then suddenly, the African-American is seen as the aggressor creating a hostile environment, rather than being supported through the hurtful process of experiencing racism and gathering the courage to call for it to cease. Blacks have to be careful how they use the term racism in the workplace, unless they have a legal caseload of unambiguous evidence to prove it. Otherwise, they become the paranoid schizophrenic at work. When African-Americans attempt to remove themselves from this unfortunate racist's environment by being standoffish, they become the topic of work gossip.

Many companies that want to avoid addressing or acknowledging racism towards African-Americans try to dig up things wrong with the work performance that would legitimize their termination and avoid a racially motivated discrimination lawsuit. Most employers and employees think of diversity training as a joke and something that they don't need. Employers need to train their employees on how to interact with other races.

Company or organization leaders (overwhelmingly White men) tend to select, groom, and promote individuals who remind them of themselves. Unconscious bias blinds them to prospective leaders who don't look, act, or sound like they do. Many times, the Caucasians that Black leaders appoint to their leadership circle create an illusion that the Black leaders are monstrous. This is so that others employees will keep their distance, and the Black leadership has no clue of the discrepancies of lower level employees. It's also their way of achieving job security for themselves.

African-Americans must change the lens through which company leadership sees them. I suggest holding your head up high and acting like you own the place. Being deferential does not increase your likability. It just feeds the perception that you lack the knowledge for the matter at hand. Express yourself boldly if you have an opinion or a position. This means that you shouldn't keep your good ideas to yourself around executive leadership at meetings. Of course, they will get challenged persistently. Even after they've proven their worth over and over again, they'll still get challenged.

How Blacks Perceive Themselves in the Work Environment

- It is assumed that their questions mean they're oblivious or the conversation is above their head.
- Separation is perceived as defiance.
- Pride for one's race makes them, "TOO BLACK."
- Their advancement in a company is considered a result of favoritism, affirmative action, blackmail, or sexual deeds.
- Their confidence is perceived as arrogance.
- Their intelligence is minimized to "Having potential."
- Their kindness is taken for a weakness.
- Their mistakes are seen as being the result of being overwhelmed.
- Their silence is taken as a lack of knowledge in the matter being discussed.
- Their uniqueness is considered strange. (*Hair Style, Fashion Trends*)
- Their accomplishments are assumed to have occurred by accident.
- Their vernacular is perceived as slang or street.
- To voice concern is discontentment.

The Problems that Come with Being "Black" in the Work Environment

- You are told your attitude is affecting others. You are asked to...."lighten up, not be so serious about the work. Smile and laugh more often, to make others more comfortable working with you."

- After a staff meeting, your boss suggests, "you need to work at making others more comfortable with you...why don't you smile more often?"

- You continually get more responsibility, but no authority.

- You realize that at times you must "dumb down" appearing to be dependent and unaware, so that your manager and peers feel they are helping you...

- A colleague says with a broad smile, "You know, I really like you. When I see you, I don't see color. I don't think of you as Black."

- You are frequently asked why you change your hairstyle so often.

- You tell your manager about a racial problem you are having and the response you get is, "You've got to be exaggerating! I find that hard to believe."

- Your first name is arbitrarily shortened to one or two syllables without your permission.

- You have to work harder than your Caucasian colleagues, just so you can be noticed.

- Walking through the hall with colleagues, you exchange greetings with two other Blacks you pass along the way. Your colleague says in amazement, "My you know so many people."

- You have to document everything.

Types of African-American employees:

- **The "Work Horse" Type:** These African-Americans have been hearing the same line from supervisors for years: "You have so much potential." Yet, they are never given an opportunity to advance in their careers. They are always given more responsibility, but rarely receive more financial compensation/raises. Unfortunately, they will always hold a mediocre job at their respective place of employment. They will seldom advance out of their current role, because they're so good at what they do. Employers do not want to go through the hassle of finding, hiring, or training someone else to do their position.

Employers realize that these individuals are an invaluable asset to the company. Yet, the employer will rarely praise them. The "Work horse" thinks their appreciated and valued. They are extremely loyal to their employers. These are the kinds of individuals who are willing to work endless hours, realizing someone will take credit for their hard work. Their supervisors often take credit for their outstanding work, seemingly because they know they can get away with it. The "Work horse" will not confront those taking advantage of them, because they feel "lucky" to have a job. They don't realize that their employer is "lucky" to have them. Yet, their supervisors are aware of their perception. The "Work horse" is the type of African-American that thinks the company will be loyal to them if they're loyal to it.

- **The "Black Power" Type**: These are the African-Americans that are extremely Afrocentric. They even dress in traditional African attire occasionally. They're all about Black pride. The "Black Power" type makes every issue or discrepancy about race. Their personality developed because they have been a victim of racism. Therefore, they hang on to the constant pain of their experience. The "Black Power" type view their pain as a strength or attribute to recognize racist propaganda in all aspects of life. The "Black Power" type is seldom liked by any other ethnic group in the work environment.

- **The "Irrational" Type:** These African-Americans are perceived as the loose cannons. Most people in the work environment assume they're "crazy." They may very well have mental health issues. Employers overlook what these individuals say or do, because they're presumed to have a mental health disability. Companies rarely fire these African-Americans, in fear of litigation. They will never advance past their current position.

- **The "Exaggeratedly Religious" Type:** They hide behind their religion while making the work environment hostile. These African-Americans are quick to pass judgement on others. They perceive themselves to be better and more consciously aware of the spiritual realm of life.

- **The "Company Owes Me" Type:** These African-Americans used to be outstanding and dedicated workers. They know the ins and outs of the trade. Now, they do just enough to make the work day pass. They are often close to retirement age, and have very little to show for their years of service. They feel as if the company has taken advantage of them, throughout the years.

- **The "I Don't Need to Work" Type:** These African-Americans have a lot of bluster around other Black employees, but are the biggest cowards around Caucasians. When Caucasian supervisors approach them, they're the first to run up to them with a big smile and ask what needs to be done and how to do it. Around other Blacks, they claim they don't have to work, but show up to work faithfully every day. They want other Blacks to think they're "Big Shots," when in truth, they do not have a proverbial "Pot to Piss In."

- **The "Want to be Everyone's Friend" Type:** These African-Americans have no shame when it comes to telling everyone's business. They spread gossip and rumors. These are the individuals that "Kiss up" to everyone in the work environment. They're always attempting to find a person's weakness. Casual conversations lead to questions that are aimed at prying information from individuals for malicious intent. They're always looking for some kind of weakness to use to their advantage. To be accepted by others, they often make themselves be whatever people want them to be.

- **The "I'm Better Than You" Type**: These African-Americans are the ones that feel the job is beneath them. They have credentials or years of experience in a specific area of expertise, but currently have a low level position at the company. The "I'm better than you" type, often feels they know more than their superiors. They resent their current status in life. They come to work thinking they're too good for their job. They are constantly frustrated, believing they're not using their skills or living up to their potential.

- **The "By Any Means Necessary" Type:** These African-Americans are willing to do anything to get to the top. These are the kind of African-Americans, who are willing to throw other Blacks under the bus to get ahead. If they're given a leadership position, it's simply because they've demonstrated extreme loyalty and a willingness to keep others Blacks in line.

- **The "Bitter" Type:** These are the kind of African-Americans that are always on the lookout to sabotage other Blacks who aspire to advance in the company. They complain about everything and don't hesitate to point the finger at others when things go wrong. They often love to point out, "What's not their job" or "how they don't pay me enough to do ….."

- **The "Rebel" Type:** These are the kind of African-Americans that perceive themselves as one of the few Blacks at the company who has the guts to tell Whites how he or she really feels. The "Rebel" type mistakes outspokenness for courage.

- **The "Timid" Type:** These are the kind of African-Americans scared of Whites and that's why they're motivated to do their job well. Because of their idealized mindset, they've been placed in supervisory positions over other Blacks. These are the types that tell Whites about what other Blacks are saying behind closed doors. Any information they find out about another Black person, they will tell. The "Timid" type is more likely to support a man of another race at a workplace than an African-American. They are more than likely to help create and enforce institutionally racist business policies that keep other Blacks down. They're the ones to laugh with Whites who laugh at him. They have no dignity. No shame. No self-respect.

- **The "Refusal to See Discrimination" Type:** These are the totally clueless Blacks who believe in the ideals of the "American Dream." They see themselves as the individuals who have pulled themselves up by their bootstraps. They think there is no racism in the world and believe in the "rainbow" and the "Great American melting pot." In their eyes, Blacks have the same privileges and advantages as Whites.

- **The "Work is My Life" Type:** These are the individuals that have no nuclear family. They hide behind their work to justify being lonely. They've put their careers before everything and now work is all they truly possess, along with material items.

- **The "Scarred" Type:** These were once the enthusiastic and eager people at work. They decided to make a good name for themselves at the company. They used to be amongst the hardest workers at the company. They've been looked over and passed over for leadership and growth opportunities at work. They have lost their ambition.

- **The "Used" Type:** They'll do a good job for the company, but they're not interested in getting ahead there. They're just interested in getting paid.

- **The "I'm Here Until Something Better Comes Along" Type:** These employees do just enough to get by. They're just buying their time and collecting a check. No goals. No purpose. They've mentally checked out. They no longer take initiative. They have quit attempting to get better.

- **The "I Want to Be or Think I'm in Charge" Type**: These African-Americans are notoriously insecure and fear any competition coming from another Black. They will bully and threaten other Blacks under their supervision or who they work with. They are negative, narcissistic, selfish, and want to have total control. Too full of themselves. They will continually point the guilty finger at others.

- **The "Visionary" Type**: These African-Americans take action and finish, even when failure appears likely. They won't take "No" for an answer. They have strong work ethics and are very ambitious. They see opportunities for growth and take advantage of them. They refuse to let others take advantage of their genius. They remain positive and create a productive work environment for themselves. They see people for who they are and adjust their attitude accordingly.

Chapter 7:
Money Matters

"At the bottom of education, at the bottom of politics, even at the bottom of religion, there must be for our race economic independence." (Booker T. Washington)

Many African-Americans fall short of the American Dream. Racial disparities in education, employment, and wealth remain drivers of inequity. It often seems that the American dream was created for Caucasians. The American dream seems to elude many African-Americans, regardless of how hard they chase after it. How can the American Dream be achieved if not every human being has the same equal opportunities as the person standing next to them? Until there is an end to discrimination and everyone is viewed as equals, the American Dream will never truly exist for some. The media portrays that everyone has equal access to the American Dream, but behind the scenes, color lines still play a role with how easily access to the American dream is obtained and who has access. This wide disparity reflects limited African-American family assets, lower rates of home ownership, limited savings, and few investments. In the story of the American Dream, education and a good job are supposed to erase the class differences into which we are born and open opportunity to anyone with ability and determination, regardless of race.

Some African-Americans get lucky. They have Caucasians in their corner willing to help make the road to success a little easier. But the majority of African-Americans will have to learn how to sell themselves, so they can reach the pinnacle of success on their own. I'm not saying that every Caucasian is born with a silver spoon in their mouth. I know Caucasians that struggle to make ends meet like many Black families. They are born in America with a certain degree of privilege. Their skin color allows them to avoid certain challenges or obstacles.

Why Money Matters

It's no secret that the dominant culture in America is more tolerant of minorities with money. Money changes the face of racism. Publicly, many Caucasians assert they are fine with intertwining their culture with other ethnic groups such as African-Americans. Yet, studies show that even those Caucasians that claim they are not racist exhibit racist, prejudice, or discriminatory tendencies when those outside their race affected their personal lives. If their children became intimately involved in a relationship with someone from another race or if someone of another race received a career advance or recognition over them, they demonstrate these biased tendencies. Wealth changes the attitude and perspective of racism. For example, even those Caucasian parents who are racist at heart are tolerant of their children dating or marrying minorities that are financially well-off. We see this example often with millionaire professional athletes, actors/actresses, and entertainers.

Gaps in wealth, not in education, between African-Americans and Caucasian families may be the most powerful force locking Americans into their social class. This division can be attributed to the incongruities in inheritance. The overall distribution of wealth is troubling. African-Americans, a group that is thirteen percent of the U.S. population and built one of the wealthiest countries the world has known through slave labor, controls less than 1.75 percent of that country's household wealth. (Pew Research Study) Caucasian families hold ninety percent of the national wealth. Wealth provides financial security, bestows social prestige, contributes to political power, and can be used to produce more wealth.

The Bible states in Proverbs 13:22 that *"A good man leaveth an inheritance to his children's children."*

Wealth inequality has been structured over many generations through the same systemic barriers that have hampered African-Americans throughout their history in American society: slavery, Jim Crow, discrimination, and institutionalized racism. For African-Americans, the damage has not only been the loss of life and property over the ages, but also the loss of opportunity to prosper in a networked environment and the lost inheritance of future generations. Rev. Dr. Martin Luther King Jr. projected that a mass wealth building program was needed in America. His proposals called for mass federal investment into the poor and working class of America to secure jobs, housing, and the opportunity to build wealth for all Americans.

The median net worth of Caucasians is about ten times more than that of African-Americans. Darrick Hamilton, PhD, a New School economist revealed these figures using Census Department data, along with Duke University's William Darity, Jr, PhD and Rebecca Tippett, PhD at the University of North Carolina. African-Americans with college degrees have less in savings and other assets than Caucasian-Americans who dropped out of high school. According to a recent calculation, the median household headed by an African-American college graduate had about two-thirds of the net worth of the median Caucasian household headed by someone who did not finish high school. On average, Caucasian households have thirteen times the wealth of African-American households, according to the Pew Research Center. The gap is growing. Wealth assets, like homes, stocks, or retirement accounts, minus debts are even more heavily concentrated in the hands of a very small number of rich Americans.

A Piece of the Pie

When new immigrants come to America and are given exceptional treatment or privileges, such as tax breaks or incentives, many African-Americans view them as sort of cutting in line or taking advantage of the system. These immigrants receive incentives not afforded to African-Americans, whereas the very economic standing of America was built on the backs, sweat, and tears of their African ancestors. African-Americans have feelings of resentment, because it appears as if these immigrants are encouraged and granted the resources to obtain the middle-class lifestyle or higher. Whereas African-Americans, who were here first and whose ancestors went through years of persecution and discrimination, are expected to recover from years of subjugation and improve their class status on their own. They are forced to ignore the residual effects of their forefathers' or foremothers' oppression.

Ironically, African-Americans are expected to improve class status by the same means as their Caucasians counterparts. Nevertheless, Caucasians have had an unfair advantage, due to generations of accumulated wealth by their ancestors. This is the real calamity of slave descendants in America. You can't find finite data for the intangible damage of this immeasurable plight. This is a persistent effect, compounded with very real systemic discrimination, that doesn't just go away when progressive America delights itself on discourse about discrimination. I think the effects of years of oppression have contributed to the huge gaps in economic status.

In my opinion, reparations don't necessarily mean giving all African-Americans a check for hundreds or thousands of dollars in the mail each month. Reparations could include placing money into school systems with predominantly Black populations to address the inequities in educational resources. Let's put money into programs that support children who are born into economically challenged neighborhoods, so they will have the opportunity to go to school, attend college, and obtain a well-paid career.

There have already been five major waves of political activism that have promoted the idea of reparations for African Americans since the emancipation of slaves: (1) the Civil War Reconstruction Era; (2) the turn of the twentieth century; (3) the Garvey movement; (4) the Civil Rights movement; and (5) the resurgence of efforts following the Civil Liberties Act of 1988. All have been unsuccessful, because reparations for African-Americans are a touchy subject. The fifteen nations of the Caribbean have sued Spain, Portugal, the Netherlands, England for the unconscionable wealth they gained trading Black slaves.

Learn About Money

I would argue that the obstacle of social class is bigger than that of race. It seems that no matter your race, humans have a desire to have what others in their class consider unattainable. Many African-Americans still think that having a Mercedes, BMW, Lexus, or a big house gives them "status" or that they have achieved the American Dream. Blacks continue to show off to each other, yet fail to encourage, teach, or share the secrets of their success with other African-Americans. They refuse to see that they are no better because of what they own. In fact, most of them are one or two paychecks away from poverty.

Growing up middle-class, I didn't understand anything about the idea of investing money to make money work for me. My family lived paycheck to paycheck. We spent what we had. When we got more, we spent more. One of the reasons the rich get richer, the poor get poorer, and the middle-class struggles in debt is that the subject of money is taught at home, not in school.

"Schools focus on scholastic and professional skills, but not on financial skills. This explains how smart bankers, doctors and accountants who earned excellent grades in school may still struggle financially all of their lives." (Robert T. Kiyosaki)

124

Most of us learn about money from our parents. So what can a poor parent tell their child about money? They simply say, "Stay in school and study hard." The child may graduate with excellent grades, but will have a poor person's financial programming and mindset. What you think is what you do. Some of us have a poverty mentality, because we didn't grow up with anything so when we do gain, we fear that we might lose it, so we hold on to everything.

It would make sense that in a world ruled by the power of currency, finances would be an essential part of the public educational curriculum. The public school system is not designed to teach anyone how to achieve financial success. Students spend most of their class hours learning information that has very limited value as it relates to acquiring future financial wealth. Those students that don't have anyone at home to teach them how to acquire wealth will have to learn money management on their own. Those upper-class bureaucrats in power realize this disadvantage and are content. They are content, because the balance of power remains in their favor.

When it comes to building wealth, debt levels matter. Most people don't know where their money goes. That's why it's important to keep track of your monthly expenditures. Once you know where your money is going, then you can decide where you need to make cutbacks. There's a false belief that someone can be debt-free. There is no such thing as being debt-free. Rich people simply know how to manage their debt. Create a workable budget for yourself. Separate your expenses into "needs" and "wants." Break up your take-home pay as follows: sixty-five percent toward things you need, including groceries, rent or mortgage, utilities and transportation; twenty percent toward savings and debt reduction, and fifteen percent toward things you want (such as vacations and going out with friends). That way, you can take care of your obligations and still enjoy life.

We all know people who spend more than they have. They get into debt using credit to purchase things they can't afford. According to "The African American Financial Experience," a survey study released by Prudential Financial, sixty percent of African-Americans surveyed have significant credit card debt versus forty-five percent of the general population. Most people end up paying interest on their interest if they carry a balance over the long-term. When you budget, you have a sense that you can afford to live the way you want to live, and therefore you can enjoy it. You don't worry, because you know you can afford it. It is important to determine your level of financial satisfaction. If you feel you could be living differently or struggling less, ask yourself what you need to do to change things. Be willing to work to make things better or different. You were meant to enjoy the fruits of your labor. Debt never made anyone happy.

Ask yourself: can you financially afford the things you want? Does your career offer you the opportunity to afford the things you want? If not, you need to reexamine your career and your materialistic desires. There's nothing wrong with wanting and enjoying material things, but just make sure you can afford them.

One of the biggest mistakes most African-Americans encounter is that they are living check to check and don't have funds stored for an emergency or a "rainy day." Most African-Americans have little financial cushion to absorb the impact of social, legal, or health-related adversity. The earnings gap between the races makes it harder for African-Americans to save. Most financial planners advise that emergency savings should be a top priority, even before retirement savings. Prudential's study found that having "emergency savings" was the third priority for most African-Americans after paying down debt and saving for retirement. It's important to have three months' worth of cash in savings for emergencies—six months if you are self-employed.

The Prudential study affirms that African-Americans aren't saving their money. Sixty percent of African-Americans they surveyed stated that they had less than $50,000 in company retirement plans and only twenty-three percent have more than $100,000. The study also discovered that African-Americans are three times more likely to tap into our 401(k) plans during difficult financial times. The study found that African-Americans retire earlier than the general population on average, despite significantly lower retirement savings. African-Americans are also retiring with insufficient financial cushioning than other average ethnic groups. That occurs even if they participate in 401(k)s and other retirement accounts.

The typical Caucasian family in their sixties has $285,000 more in wealth than their African-Americans counterpart. That means Caucasians are better able to enjoy a comfortable retirement and pass along wealth to the next generation of heirs (children and grandchildren) so that they can have a head start in life and use their families' wealth to pay for college, invest, start businesses, or buy homes. Often times, African-American families are in so much debt that their parents aren't able to financially assist in any way to help their children. Federal government programs aimed at helping Americans buy homes and save for retirement rely on tax breaks and aren't as available to African-Americans, who characteristically have lower incomes. The bottom twenty percent of taxpayers, in terms of income, received less than one percent of federal subsidies for homeownership or retirement.

A study, done by Credit Suisse in conjunction with the Institute on Assets and Social Policy at Brandeis University, found that the wealthiest five percent of African-Americans, those with a net worth of $357,000 or better, dispense a greater share of their holdings into relatively low-risk, low-reward investment vehicles, such as certificates of deposit, saving bonds, and insurance policies, rather than stocks, bonds and mutual funds. Those well-off African-Americans tend to have more of their wealth in real estate.

Your Dream

The survey found that African-Americans are nearly twice as likely as others to have a dream of starting a small business and believe this will allow them to have financial stability and freedom. However, they noted that they lacked significant capital to make their dream a reality. Studies found that African-

American entrepreneurs receive bank loans with less frequency, of smaller size, and at higher interest rates than Caucasian-owned companies. Access to capital, clientele, and other resources hinder many African-American from starting businesses. Other ethnic groups have learned to pool their resources together. They start their own lending institutions, invest money into each other's business, and teach others from their culture how to make money. Yet, African-Americans have fallen behind in this understanding.

Although African-Americans make up approximately thirteen percent of the U.S. population, African-Americans own just seven percent of small businesses. African-American buying power is around a trillion dollars, yet less than three cents of every dollar an African-American spends in this country goes to Black-owned businesses. African-Americans have allowed other ethnic groups to capitalize off of their ingenuity through poverty. For *example, consider soul food, fashion, and music.* The NAACP reported, that a dollar circulates in Asian communities for a month, in Jewish communities *approximately* twenty days, in Caucasian communities seventeen days, and in Black communities six hours. African-American business owners commonly state that there is a lack of support from the Black community.

I know this is a bold assertion, but African-Americans are one of the few races that neglect to support those from their own race. The perceived fear is that the African-Americans they assist may prevail or exceed their own circumstances. Some African-Americans have a "crab in a barrel" mindset. When one African-American moves to the top, there is another Black ready to pull them down, similar to crabs in a barrel. It's a selfish mentality ingrained in the minds of Blacks since slavery. This is a problematic mentality that must be broken if African-Americans want to progress.

"If we do not hang together, we shall surely hang separately". (Thomas Paine)

I have done numerous seminars at predominately Black churches, HBCU's, and minority organizations around the country. In many instances, I've done seminars for free or given discounts, because the need for these events is important in strengthening the Black community. It's disheartening to see the lack of interest or willingness to invest in finding solutions to change current circumstances. African-Americans will applaud my message, invite me to speak and attend other events, and praise my efforts. Yet, when I ask them to buy copies of my books or attend one of my larger reasonably-priced paid conferences, a look of reluctance appears on their faces.

Everything has a cost and facilities and guest speakers don't come free. Typically, my seminars or conferences are cheaper than most, considering I understand the burdens of monetary strain. My mission was never to become rich from God's mandate for my life. My financial blessing comes from other gifts and avenues. I learned some time ago that people put money into things they hold of value.

Desegregation was one of the best and worst things to happen to African-Americans. Desegregation had nothing to do with the government's desire for social reform. It was more about America gaining and maintaining their position as an economic powerhouse. Desegregation resulted in African-Americans attempting to gain Caucasian acceptance. At the threshold of desegregation, African-Americans wanted to exercise their new freedoms, so they attempted to prove their equivalency to Caucasians through their purchasing power. African-Americans no longer viewed Black-owned businesses as suitable or up to standard. It's the typical "grass is greener on the other side" scenario. This also explains why African-Americans moved and still move out of predominantly Black neighbors today; it's no longer viewed as adequate.

African-American customers don't properly invest in Black businesses. African-American customers often expect discounts, because of the patronizing a

Black business. (These are discounts they wouldn't expect from business owners of another race.) Owning a business is not an easy task, especially if you're African-American. Many small Black-owned businesses fail within their first year. Yet even with this knowledge, you wouldn't believe the number of African-American customers who expect, or in some cases demand, special treatment when it comes to pricing.

Before Black businesses can get off the ground well enough, African-American customers want goods or services for a discount or for free. Black business owners appreciate African-American support, and I imagine they would provide discounts or freebies if they could. I can't tell you how many times I've visited a small Black-owned business and seen someone approach the checkout counter and attempted to talk their way into a discount or "hookup." African-American customers must remember, Black business owners are doing everything they can to make their business a success. Like so many of us, they have financial obligations to their families.

Some relationships turn bitter when people get angry at not receiving perks. I don't think Black business owners are trying to be cruel when they shy away from discounts or freebie requests. Perhaps times are slow and they really need the money.

Ironically, Black consumers argue that African-American business prices are higher than other ethnic groups. African-Americans in positions of authority in financial institutions are more inclined to give money or loans to other ethnic groups than those from their own race. It is perceived that African-Americans are less likely to pay back loans. It's unfortunate that when many African-Americans get in a position of authority or in a leadership position, they are fearful of helping other Blacks advance. Many African-Americans fear that someone observing them would suggest that they unfairly helped another African-American, because of the color of their skin. I even notice this trend as it relates to hiring African-Americans for employment opportunities.

Higher Paying Jobs

It's perceived by African-Americans that they aren't even considered for high paying employment opportunities unless they're overqualified. According to many African-Americans, Caucasians with simply a certification, diplomas, associate's degree or bachelor's degree can assume higher or the same types of employment as African-Americans who hold higher degrees such as master's or doctoral degrees. Not only are Caucasians able to acquire these career opportunities, but their pay is typically equal or higher than African-Americans with those terminal degrees.

African-Americans criticize Caucasians for feeling entitled to higher paying jobs or leadership positions, especially if they possess a college degree. It's perceived by African-Americans that Caucasians will not accept anything less. Even if they are completely unqualified for a position, those in power are willing to train them. Further, due to their insistence for authority, those in power commend them for their willingness to purse leadership or more responsibility, denoting their attitude as ambitious or career-driven.

Where's the Support?

W.E.B. Du Bois's analogy of the "Talented Tenth" describes the innate division we still witness in Black culture today. Du Bois stated the "Talented Tenth" was the segment of African-Americans that had achieved some level of success. Instead of helping the other segment of African-Americans so they could also achieve a better life, the "Talented Tenth" would choose to look down on their people or aid them in a condescending manner.

Wealthy African-Americans today are paid well enough so that they can ignore racial issues. They are coerced by their financial power to give diplomatic answers so that they don't offend anyone, even when they know an act towards an

African-American is truly unjust and racially motivated. They standby idly, because they fear that they will lose their favor in the Caucasian community, instead of supporting the Black community.

Dr. Umar Johnson, a Doctor of Clinical Psychology and a National Certified School Psychologist, stated in an interview that wealthy African-Americans during the Civil Rights era regularly spoke up for the Black community. This was because wealthy African-Americans still lived in the same neighborhoods as every other Black due to segregation laws. Therefore, wealthy African-Americans could not avoid their responsibility to their Black communities. As wealthy African-Americans in entertainment and sports gained more appeal and influence in White and Black communities, those Caucasians in power sought to capitalize off of their reputable impact.

The effort started with separating wealthy African-Americans from the Black community; it's "Divide and Conquer," so to speak. If the Black community remained their power base, then these wealthy African-Americans would remain loyal to Black people. As these African-Americans became wealthier, so would the Black community. Having a wealthy Black community was something these Caucasians in power would not permit. Therefore, a situation was created so that the power base would shift. The Caucasian population would now show favor, support, and financially contribute to the success of these wealthy African-Americans. If you look today, Caucasians are now the major financial power base behind wealthy Blacks. Those Caucasians in power have made wealthy African-Americans totally dependent on them. Hence, it makes wealthy African-Americans think twice before they speak out against racial injustice to Blacks when their career or financial stability is on the line.

The question becomes, if wealthy African-Americans did acknowledge racism in America and spoke out against it, how many African-Americans would protect or support them? It's no secret that African-Americans fail to support or protect their own. African-Americans will rally with an individual and agree with concerns or issues behind closed doors. Yet, when it becomes time to voice their concerns to the source, only a few, if any, will stand with that individual. It's not uncommon for the one that finds him or herself standing alone to become the martyr for the cause. Unfortunately, it's the people that fail to stand up that often times benefit from the efforts of one.

Financial Pitfalls and Family Obligations

African-American families with some wealth are often compelled to use those extra dollars to make up for longstanding economic gaps by supporting relatives who lack savings. According to Prudential's African-American Financial Experience study, Black families are often financially responsible for family members. Loaning money to family and friends instead of saving or paying down debt is a financial mistake. Consider ways to help out your relatives rather than giving them money. If you do decide to loan family money, the smart thing to do is to put everything in writing and decide on a reasonable repayment plan. If they fail to pay you back on time, they've made it easy to say 'No' the next time they asked.

Most African-Americans are descendants of deeply impoverished rural agricultural workers, so they can expect to borrow only small sums from relatives and can expect only small inheritances. According to a study from the Institute on Assets and Social Policy at Brandeis University, nearly half of White households received financial transfers from other relatives. The median amount of that movement of intra-family wealth was $83,692. Just one tenth of African-American households, meanwhile, received money or other assets from relatives, and among these few, the median amount was $52,240.

Inheritance plays a critical role in the wealth gap. Caucasians are five times more likely to receive large gifts or inheritances. African-Americans need to do a better job preparing for death. Even when African-Americans have adequately prepared for death, their reluctance to disclose personal information to trusted family members eventually poses issues. Family members find themselves in a position of attempting to locate important papers to verify insurance coverage or a last will and testament. If these items can't be found, this places a burden on the family and friends to cover funeral arrangements. It's upsetting to witness African-American families having to resort to asking for donations, because the deceased didn't have their affairs in order.

I've also seen when the opposite occurs, when loved one's refuse to acknowledge or listen to an individual's provisions for death. The topic of death is typically not a preferred conversation piece in the Black community. In fact, it often seems taboo to discuss one's own demise in many regards. The consequence of this lack of communication leaves families and loved ones unprepared and frustrated once the person is deceased.

According to LexisNexis, sixty-eight percent of African-Americans don't have a will or estate plan, regardless of how painful the idea of death may be. The reality is that we will all die some day. Protect your dependents: your kids, spouse and parents. Remember that life insurance can also help defray costs and pay off any debt not discharged by death. Start by checking with your employer to see if they provide life insurance and how much. If that's not an option, go get term life insurance. It is cheap and simple. Minimally, African-Americans should have enough to cover any debts, including your mortgage and have enough to support your spouse and children until they reach adulthood.

If African-Americans are vested in getting out of debt so that they can pass wealth to their children, they should consider universal methods of outreach such as helping them take concrete steps toward financial security. African-Americans should pull their credit report and get their FICO score every four months. Consolidate student loans and review insurance plans for cheaper rates. Negotiate for lower interest rates on credit cards. Cut back on discretionary expenses, including dining out. Keep credit card balances low. If the temptation of using your credit card seems too much for you to resist, cut it, but don't close the accounts. It's not so much that opportunity creates wealth, but that wealth creates opportunity.

Chapter 8:
Defining Your Sense of Worth and Value

African-Americans have to express greatness every time an opportunity presents itself. In the case of African-Americans who have faced and continue to face prejudice and discrimination, they have to instill pride in their children and teach them about their culture and history. This will allow them to combat the negative images and perceptions about themselves. When people look at African-Americans, they are looking at a unique manifestation of the almighty creator's love. African-American males should believe they are number one and act like it.

African-American males have been incredibly creative in finding ways to adapt to society's demands. All their lives African-Americans have been told how to assimilate themselves into Caucasian society, so they can be accepted as equals. Yet, Caucasians have failed to fully adapt to their presence.

America has always defined the male role as that of protector and provider, but the African-American male is, in many cases, incapable of playing that role for a number of reasons. Lack of job opportunities or career advancements can diminish the self-confidence and ego of African-American men, because their perceived role as family provider or independence is stripped. While he may understand that racism is frequently the cause of his failure, the Black male's structured inability to play his role can take a psychological toll. Lack of job opportunities leads individuals to engage in illegal activities to generate income. On a global scale, the image of the African-American male has been emasculated. His image in the eyes of African-American women and children of color has diminished. This is identifiable with the African-American male's position in slavery.

A male in a position of authority is more appealing than a male who is not. Many African-American men would argue that successful women of color tend to overlook African-American men who make less money or have honest hardworking careers that are deemed less than desirable in public opinion. Since the unemployment rate is traditionally higher in the Black community, many African-American men accept jobs that call for them to work under very hazardous conditions or positions where they are overqualified.

Successful African-American women often times find themselves in relationships with men of other ethnic groups, because African-American men are generally not in their upper social or professional circle. What are the chances of a successful African-American female CEO pursuing a relationship with a Black male that has a career as a custodian? How would her fellow colleagues perceive her once his occupation was disclosed? The statement of 'she's out of your league' certainly holds merit. Psychologically, people are attracted to power.

I think America places too much of a concern on a person's job title rather than determine an individual's importance and position based on other factors. We've let those in power decide for us what is and what is not an important profession. Exposure to other people's ideas and attitudes and, in many cases, a lack of positive input can make us insecure. Oftentimes, employers are more inclined to hire African-American females over African-American males; they attempt to hire a female minority from two underrepresented groups with one hire. We are led to believe that: a doctor is more important than a factory worker; a teacher is more important than a maintenance worker or janitor; and a woman who has a nine-to-five career is more important than a woman who is a homemaker and mother. If we buy into this philosophy, we will spend our lives trying to become what "they" accept. No one can make you feel inferior without your consent.

It amazes me how often I'm introduced to someone and in the process I immediately learn where they work, what they do for a living, or their title. Never define yourself by your occupation. It's what you do. It's not who you are. African-Americans perceive that Caucasians often times define themselves by their occupations. When they introduce themselves or refer to relatives, they commonly state their occupation. This is a tendency that escapes African-Americans. I think this tendency developed from Caucasians having occupations they could be proud of traditionally. During the early parts of American history, African-Americans were denied certain employment opportunities and took whatever job allowed them to make ends meet for their families. They realized that their occupation had nothing to do with their education or identity; it was simply a respectable job lacking a sense of pride.

The problem some African-Americans face is the belief that they're too "Black" to pursue career opportunities. When certain African-Americans get hired in careers traditionally dominated by Caucasian, they're deemed as "sellouts." The world, it seems, continually gives us the message that our worth and value are connected to our "doing" not to "who we are." Our worth and value are not based on what we do, but how well we perform what we do and how we live by our values.

A janitorial position may not have the fanciest title or be recognized as a glamorous position, but it's an honest and certainly an important position. Americans need to stop determining a person's sense of value or worth by what they do. Instead, Americans can determine a person's sense of worth better by who a person is based on their values and actions.

Americans have placed titles on ourselves and defined our existence and who we are by these titles. Everyone is not meant to be a doctor, lawyer, engineer, or pastor. Each role in life has expectations attached to it, but we must be sure whose expectations they are. Don't let your occupation define who you are either. Sometimes, we think having a certain position will give us power, when, in reality, the position may end up having power over us.

In an earlier chapter, I mentioned the need for approval. Some people become approval addicts, always needing the approval of others to be happy and secure. Many people have a poor self-image and they try to enhance their image through positions. People are going to talk regardless, whether you give them a reason or not. Don't worry about it. Your existence doesn't rely on their approval or disapproval. Be happy and confident in yourself. Trying to live up to everyone's rules, customs, and expectations is a no-win situation. The only person you should be competing against is yourself. Comparing yourself and your success to someone else's is unfair to you, because you don't know the advantages or disadvantages the other person(s) encountered. Nothing will create more frustration in you than trying to live your life to please other people. You shouldn't be concerned about what other people think.

"The hardest challenge is to be yourself in a world where everyone is trying to make you be somebody else." (E. E. Cummings)

Self-confidence allows us to have a positive and realistic perception of our abilities and ourselves. We're not going to make everyone happy. We have to accept responsibility for our own lives and actions.

"Whoever you are, there is some younger person who thinks you are perfect. There is some work that will never be done if you don't do it. There is someone who would miss you if you were gone. There is a place that you alone can fill." (Jacob M. Braude)

Chapter 9:
Men of Action, "Walking in the Glory of Success"

When you live out the beauty of your purpose, it gives the rest of the world an opportunity to witness your exquisiteness. You don't have to be perfect, but you have to give perfect effort. Many of our young African-American males are confused. They believe that because they are special the road to success should be or will be easy. To realize your purpose, your being special alone won't help you achieve your goal. The rest of the world responds to your exquisiteness when you earn it.

Stop envisioning the type of success that is inconsistent with who you are. Most people spend much of their lives desiring and attempting to "fit in," but as a result we fail to standout. Ironically, it's not our fault, because we've been conditioned to think this way. Whenever we decide to step outside the parameters that society deems ordinary, we're labeled as radical. Ironically, radical thinkers are later considered innovators. We've been conditioned to be ordinary.

Many of us want what great looks like, but too few are willing to do what greatness requires. If you're going to be successful, you're going to experience what it's like to feel discomfort. Balance is difficult when striving for success. When you give in one area, you sacrifice in another. That's where our spirituality compensates. Greatness is not a destination; it's a persistent journey. If you have read this and are comfortable, then you have not learned the path to greatness. Greatness is not a job; it's not a single opportunity. Greatness is a persistent effort given to many opportunities.

Those that are great will deny their greatness, but explain that they have simply made it their mission to attempt to outrun average. They are running in the opposite direction of being average. Never stop to dwell or pat yourself on the back. The key to greatness is to realize that you haven't done enough.

Growth is never easy and you will certainly experience growing pains. Success can be defined as experiencing the effects of your desired position. Often times, you will have to cut off those that are not going in your same direction, even if it hurts. It's one of the hazards of being the smartest person in your circle. You should not be the smartest person in your group. In that case, then you are not growing.

The only way to become great is to engage greatness. I look at people who have the life or things I want, I ask how they got it. Greatness recognizes greatness. They seek out each other. If you act as if you know everything, then they assume you don't need the information. So they don't give it to you. You must be humble enough to ask how and why. An arrogant person will look like a fool pretending they know how to do it and then make excuses why it doesn't work. People give information to those that are willing to listen. Meet people who have already done what we desire.

Every successful person you can think of has stepped outside of what was considered the normal and done what most people would suggest as radical or the impossible. The more willing you are to put yourself out there, to take chances, and to try new things, the more likely you are to experience failure. Failure is as natural as making mistakes. This will make you more resilient, less sensitive, and more appreciative of success when it does come along. Those that live being conditioned to an ordinary existence see that their minds will not let them fathom beyond the concept of what is impossible. It's because their mind defaults to accept limitations. Extraordinary thinkers view the impossible as possible.

What Does Success Mean to You? What does It Look Like?

Have you decided what success means to you? This is your life and you have a right to have the things you desire. However, you have to be realistic with yourself about what your desires are and then ask yourself what do you need financially to get the things you want. Be honest with yourself about where you want to be in life and how you intend to get there. You may find that what you think you want and what would make you happy are two different things.

We have to unclutter our lives and arrange things so we can receive change. Stop spending so much time looking at the television and waiting and watching others become successful. You should be finding ways to invest in your own success. We need to free ourselves from the distractions that compete for our energy and attention. African-Americans should use their anger to spark change. Our view of our individual circumstances will always change with our ever-changing mood and feeling level.

What chains are tying you down and preventing you from reaching your goals? Life is like standing on a crumbling cliff. You either jump or risk falling down. I would rather risk my chances jumping with a leap of faith. Pull free from old distractions. Break away from habits that sap your energy and usurp your time. No longer should we use "about to." We should be "doing." 'About to' indicates that you still haven't arrived in your personal pursuit for growth. 'About to' means that you are in the preparation stages. Simply stating that you "Tried" has never done anything for anyone. "Production" is what makes things happen.

"There are two ways of exerting one's strength: one is pushing down, the other is pulling up." (Booker T. Washington)

"Man's greatness consists in his ability to do and the proper application of his powers to things needed to be done." (Frederick Douglass)

African-Americans in Positions of Leadership

African-Americans must not be so quick to judge those Blacks in positions of authority. I commonly hear African-Americans refer to other Blacks in positions of leadership in predominately White controlled establishments as "Sellouts," "Boot Lickers," "Figure Heads," "Suck Ups," or "Uncle Toms." African-Americans often times forget that these individuals are battling the same racism and negative stereotypes they are facing. Unfortunately, as you move up the chain of command in business or educational institutions, the number of Blacks in power are drastically underrepresented. Occupational mandates on these African-Americans are particularly scrutinizing, more so than of their Caucasian colleagues. These individuals often times have to make critical decisions they may not agree with completely.

I've witnessed African-Americans get upset when Caucasians are appointed to positions of authority that they feel a Black person should rightfully occupy. They complain about the establishment being a racist institution and not allowing for career growth opportunities. Ironically, when an African-American is appointed to a position of leadership, they are upset because the African-American chosen may not be the ideal representation of what they consider it means to be "Black."

As long as these African-Americans in power are treating those they supervise equally, we should applaud their efforts. These African-Americans have financial responsibilities and their respective roles to fulfill. They are indeed a credit to their race, because there was a time Blacks could not assume these leadership roles.

Chapter 10:
What's Your Legacy?

I f you were to die tomorrow, how would you be remembered? Do you have a realistic view of the life you are living this very moment? What are your values? What do you represent? What do you want to embody? What type of interpersonal relationships are you building with others? The ultimate question is: what will be your legacy?

Dr. Ja A. Jahannes stated to me once that his success and legacy would be ingrained in the lives of the youth and students he positively affected. Mary McLeod Bethune also once stated, *"we have a powerful potential in our youth, and we must have the courage to change old ideas and practices so that we may direct their power toward good ends."* Success should breed success if African-Americans seize their moment; it lays the foundation for future generations to build upon.

Even after generations of fighting to sit in the front, African-Americans have been conditioned to take a back seat to life. African-Americans do it subconsciously without even realizing that it's the effect of generations of conditioning. Like so many young African-American men, I too used to take my conditioned position in the back seat of the classroom. Dr. Ja A. Jahannes made me realize that it was an honor and the responsibility of African-Americans to sit in the front.

"There're truths you have to grow into." (H.G. Wells)

For far too long in African-American history, Blacks have been forced to take a backseat to Caucasians, as it relates to employment, education, and basic human rights. Therefore, it's well past time for African-Americans to take their equal place up front beside other ethnic groups.

African-Americans must not be afraid to go against the restrictions imposed by fear or uncertainty. African-Americans have to allow for energy and strength to flow through them. They must have faith and act upon it. They must dare to be different from the negative images the media attempts to portray as the norm. They must stop being simply offended and become upset enough to demonstrate actions towards positive change. They must break tradition and ignore those who have set limits in their lives.

"When you do the common things in life in an uncommon way, you will command the attention of the world." (George Washington Carver)

Take charge of your life, realizing that you control your future. You don't have to violently force others to respect you. Let your good actions and the empowerment of one's self command your deserved respect. Don't let anybody or anything cloud your vision of who you are. As Booker T. Washington said, "No greater injury can be done to any youth than to let him feel that because he belongs to this or that race, or because of his color, he will be advanced in life regardless of his own merits or efforts."

The role of a male is to be an educator, a protector, a provider, and a leader. I charge all American-American males to assume their respected role. Many times African-American men don't get the support that they need from their families. Aspiring to become more or step outside what those in the family accept as the norm is difficult. I encourage our African-American young males to educate themselves about the world. It's human nature to respect someone living according to an earned discipline.

"The consummate leader cultivates the moral law, and strictly adheres to proper methods and discipline; thus it is in his power to control success." – (Sun Tzu).

Your dream tells you what you will and will not do, because it gives you a reason to keep on your journey. If you don't know where you are going, how can you possibly get there? Moreover, if you don't know where you are headed, how do you know you are in the right place now? Sometimes our dreams are as clear as our own reality. Your dream is your purpose; it's what defines you. A man without a dream or vision shall perish. Before you can think about the future, you have to realize your destiny in the future. Stay focused on the present moment. This is where you are in your life right now.

"The world makes way for the man who knows where he is going." (Ralph Waldo Emerson)

"Losing your way on a journey is unfortunate. But, losing your reason for the journey is a fate more cruel." (H.G. Wells)

Frustration and failure will result as you're pulled one way, then the other. You'll feel like you have no direction. Don't excuse yourself out of greatness. Deal with transitions in your life. How do you become confident in the midst of adversity? Believe in yourself, even if no one else does. At any given time, some will cheer you while others will taunt you; maintain your core values.

"One mark of a great soldier is that he fights on his own terms or fights not at all." (Sun Tzu)

No one else has to understand or agree with your vision. It wasn't conceived for them to decipher. If it had been, they would have received the vision as well. An impatient attitude is one of the reasons that many people never reach their full potential. Patience is vital to the development of our full potential. Not everyone can encompass your vision, so spend your time wisely and decide what is best for you. As you give, you get. With time, even a piece of coal under extreme pressure becomes a beautiful and precious diamond.

Become your own success story. It's not where you start, it's where you end. Every day you are giving your testimony. The greater the adversity a person experiences, the greater their story.

"If there is no struggle, there is no progress." (Frederick Douglass)

Turn your moment into a movement by embracing the struggle. It starts with you! *"Pursue your purpose not to make a living, but to make a life." (Dr. Morris Clarington)* Your accomplishments are not determined by income, but by your impact.

African-Americans want Caucasians to realize that they are often times not given the same opportunities as them. African-Americans want Caucasians to stop believing that they've been granted opportunities, because they've prepared for success in ways African-Americans have not. Caucasians must stop believing that, because African-Americans may not have acquired as much materialistically or have as glorious of a career as them, they aren't preparing for success. Ultimately, African-Americans want everyone to understand the harm caused by discrimination. In order to make this happen, it's everyone's responsibility, regardless of their race, color, or creed to speak out to make an impact and stand up against all acts of injustice and inequity.

"Injustice anywhere is a threat to justice everywhere." (Rev. Dr. Martin Luther King Jr.)

Being an African-American can be both a source of pride and pain. African-Americans want all ethnic groups to understand their struggle. They want the dominant culture to take the time and effort to see the world as they do. African-Americans want to be seen as people and not stereotypes.

I'm tired of all the bloodshed! My heart is strong, but it continues to be broken. I've personally known African-Americans that have been killed as a result of bigotry and hatred. African-Americans have buried too many loved ones, too soon. Now the question becomes, what are we as a community or as a country going to do to change things, so that they can get better? We need to start thinking about new concepts. Does progress mean making education or jobs more accessible to those at risk? Or does improvement mean hiring more law enforcement officers, building more prisons or jails?

A comedian once said Blacks are the only race complacent in their own demise. I dread and shudder to think that this statement may have any truth. We all must live life like a solution. We all should want our lives to be our testimony. If we don't, then the sacrifices and tears of those before us will be in vain.

Although conversations about racism are uncomfortable, they are necessary. We must all understand how we participate in the framework of racism. When it comes to closing the gap, there's a long way for us to go. Racism is a learned behavior, if it can be learned, then it can be unlearned. All lives matter, because all life is precious! May the pain of our ancestors' past bring us strength and courage during future hours of darkness.

"Dolor hic tibi proderit olim" -----"This pain will be useful to you."

I conclude with a poem, entitled: "Unchained."

<u>Unchained</u>

My strength lies in my ability to overcome adversity
I refuse to believe that the hue of my skin depicts my inadequacies in any shape, form, or
fashion,
Despite the stereotypes and propaganda that would have others believe my inferiority.
I stem from the legacy of great men and women who showed great strength and
courage amongst their enslavers
And defied death when it was the easier of their options,
Through rocky seas and chattering chains,
To be seen as half human by those who wish to enslave our freedoms.
On foot, we travel the twilight hours to the bosoms of freedom.
By no means does color measure the character of a man.
As I stand in the hub of self-doubt,
I dare not blink or tremble in the face of adversity.
I walk with pride and determination.
With each stride, I grow as a man.
I've set aside childish antics, now more focused on my duties and days ahead.
Let my strength lie in my abilities to move mountains and provoke change in the
midst of chaos.
We kneel only in the presence of God, from which we obtain our strength.
I realize that not all shackles are forged from metal or chains
Some are composed of flesh and bones
And others are crafted psychologically.
Like the smoldering blackness of smoke, we rise.
Let my voice be an instrument of power.
My words will strike a mighty blow to all things that attempt to restrict our
freedoms.
I break the shackles that bind thee.

Freedom is a mentality, so in order to be free, one must be proud and love him or herself amongst all things. In the words of historical and cultural sociologist Orlando Patterson, "*African-Americans have to strike a balance between what [he] defined as the* **catastrophic** *and the* **survivalist** *interpretations of the African-American past. The catastrophic interpretation emphasizes what has been done to Black people. It highlights the horrors of the slave trade, slavery, second-class citizenship, racism, segregation, and inequality…The survivalist interpretation, on the other hand, promotes Black achievement despite their odds."*

The End!